WA 1015700 X

£395

STUDIES IN ECONOMIC AND SOCIAL HISTORY

This series, specially commissioned by the Economic History Society,
provides a guide to the current interpretations of the key themes of
economic and social history in which advances have recently been
made or in which there has been significant debate.

Originally entitled 'Studies in Economic History', in 1974 the series
had its scope extended to include topics in social history, and the new
series title, 'Studies in Economic and Social History', signalises this
development.

The series gives readers access to the best work done, helps them to
draw their own conclusions in major fields of study, and by means of
the critical bibliography in each book guides them in the selection of
further reading. The aim is to provide a springboard to further work
rather than a set of pre-packaged conclusions or short-cuts.

ECONOMIC HISTORY SOCIETY

The Economic History Society, which numbers over 3000 members,
publishes the *Economic History Review* four times a year (free to
members) and holds an annual conference. Enquiries about membership should be addressed to the Assistant Secretary, Economic
History Society, Peterhouse, Cambridge. Full-time students may join
at special rates.

D0892747

STUDIES IN ECONOMIC AND SOCIAL HISTORY

Edited for the Economic History Society by L. A. Clarkson

PUBLISHED

W. I. Albert Latin America and the World Economy from Independence to 1930
B. W. E. Alford Depression and Recovery? British Economic Growth, 1918–1939
Michael Anderson Approaches to the History of the Western Family, 1500–1914
Michael Anderson Population Change in North-Western Europe, 1750–1850
P. J. Cain Economic Foundations of British Overseas Expansion, 1815–1914
S. D. Chapman The Cotton Industry in the Industrial Revolution
Neil Charlesworth British Rule and the Indian Economy, 1800–1914
J. A. Chartres Internal Trade in England, 1500–1700
R. A. Church The Great Victorian Boom, 1850–1873
L. A. Clarkson Proto-Industrialization: The First Phase of Industrialization?
D. C. Coleman Industry in Tudor and Stuart England
P. L. Cottrell British Overseas Investment in the Nineteenth Century
M. A. Crowther Social Policy in Britain 1914–1939
Ralph Davis English Overseas Trade, 1500–1700
Ian M. Drummond The Gold Standard and the International Monetary System
M. E. Falkus The Industrialisation of Russia, 1700–1914
Peter Fearon The Origins and Nature of the Great Slump, 1929–1932
T. R. Gourvish Railways and the British Economy, 1830–1914
Robert Gray The Aristocracy of Labour in Nineteenth-century Britain, *c.* 1850–1900
John Hatcher Plague, Population and the English Economy, 1348–1530
J. R. Hay The Origins of the Liberal Welfare Reforms, 1906–1914
R. H. Hilton The Decline of Serfdom in Medieval England
E. L. Jones The Development of English Agriculture, 1815–1973
John Lovell British Trade Unions,1875–1933
W. J. Macpherson The Economic Development of Japan, *c.*1868–1941
Donald N. McCloskey Econometric History
Hugh McLeod Religion and the Working Class in Nineteenth-Century Britain
J. D. Marshall The Old Poor Law, 1795–1834
Alan S. Milward The Economic Effects of the Two World Wars on Britain
G. E. Mingay Enclosure and the Small Farmer in the Age of the Industrial Revolution
Rosalind Mitchison British Population Change Since 1860
R. J. Morris Class and Class Consciousness in the Industrial Revolution, 1780–1850
J. Forbes Munro Britain in Tropical Africa, 1870–1960
A. E. Musson British Trade Unions, 1800–1875
Patrick K. O'Brien The Economic Effects of the American Civil War
R. B. Outhwaite Inflation in Tudor and Early Stuart England
R. J. Overy The Nazi Economic Recovery, 1932–1938
P. L. Payne British Entrepreneurship in the Nineteenth Century
G. C. Peden Keynes, The Treasury and British Economic Policy
Roy Porter Disease, Medicine and Society in England, 1550–1860
G. D. Ramsay The English Woollen Industry, 1500–1750
Elizabeth Roberts Women's Work 1840–1940
Michael E. Rose The Relief of Poverty, 1834–1914
Michael Sanderson Education, Economic Change and Society in England, 1780–1870
S. B. Saul The Myth of the Great Depression, 1873–1896
Arthur J. Taylor Laissez-faire and State Intervention in Nineteenth-century Britain
Peter Temin Causal Factors in American Economic Growth in the Nineteenth Century
Joan Thirsk England's Agricultural Regions and Agrarian History, 1500–1750
Michael Turner Enclosures in Britain, 1750–1830
Margaret Walsh The American Frontier Revisited
J. R. Ward Poverty and Progress in the Caribbean 1800–1960

OTHER TITLES ARE IN PREPARATION

Social Policy in Britain 1914–1939

Prepared for
The Economic History Society by

M. A. CROWTHER
Lecturer in Economic History
University of Glasgow

MACMILLAN
EDUCATION

1015700 X

361.61
CRO

© The Economic History Society 1988

All rights reserved. No reproduction, copy or transmission
of this publication may be made without written permission.

No paragraph of this publication may be reproduced, copied
or transmitted save with written permission or in accordance
with the provisions of the Copyright Act 1956 (as amended),
or under the terms of any licence permitting limited copying
issued by the Copyright Licensing Agency, 7 Ridgmount Street,
London WC1E 7AE.

Any person who does any unauthorised act in relation to
this publication may be liable to criminal prosecution and
civil claims for damages.

First published 1988

Published by
MACMILLAN EDUCATION LTD
Houndmills, Basingstoke, Hampshire RG21 2XS
and London
Companies and representatives
throughout the world

Printed in Hong Kong

British Library Cataloguing in Publication Data
Crowther, M. A.
Social policy in Britain 1914–1939.—
(Studies in economic and social history).
1. Great Britain—Social policy   2. Great
Britain—Politics and government—
1910–1936   3. Great Britain—Politics and
government—1936–1945
I. Title   II. Economic History Society
III. Series
361.6′1′0941   HN385
ISBN 0–333–32285–1

Series Standing Order

If you would like to receive future titles in this series as they are published,
you can make use of our standing order facility. To place a standing order
please contact your bookseller or, in case of difficulty, write to us at the
address below with your name and address and the name of the series.
Please state with which title you wish to begin your standing order. (If you
live outside the UK we may not have the rights for your area, in which case
we will forward your order to the publisher concerned.)

Customer Services Department, Macmillan Distribution Ltd
Houndmills, Basingstoke, Hampshire, RG21 2XS, England.

28.9.88 (D)

Contents

List of Tables

Acknowledgements

Particular thanks are due to Pat Thane, for reading the manuscript and giving good advice. Rodney Lowe alwo helped me with much useful information. Thanks also to many of the authors mentioned in the following pages, for sending me copies of offprints and assisting with the bibliography.

Note on References

References in the text within square brackets relate to the numbered items in the Bibliography, followed, where necessary, by the page numbers in italics, for example [1, 7–9].

The cover illustration is a cartoon by David Low entitled 'Lloyd George and the double-headed Ass', circa 1921. It is reproduced here courtesy of the artist and Mail Newspapers plc. The photograph was supplied by the Centre for the Study of Cartoons and Caricature, Canterbury.

Editor's Preface

When this series was established in 1968 the first editor, the late Professor M. W. Flinn, laid down three guiding principles. The books should be concerned with important fields of economic history; they should be surveys of the current state of scholarship rather than a vehicle for the specialist views of the authors, and above all, they were to be introductions to their subject and not 'a set of pre-packaged conclusions'. These aims were admirably fulfilled by Professor Flinn and by his successor, Professor T. C. Smout, who took over the series in 1977. As it passes to its third editor and approaches its third decade, the principles remain the same.

Nevertheless, times change, even though principles do not. The series was launched when the study of economic history was burgeoning and new findings and fresh interpretations were threatening to overwhelm students – and sometimes their teachers. The series has expanded its scope, particularly in the area of social history – although the distinction between 'economic' and 'social' is sometimes hard to recognise and even more difficult to sustain. It has also extended geographically; its roots remain firmly British, but an increasing number of titles is concerned with the economic and social history of the wider world. However, some of the early titles can no longer claim to be introductions to the current state of scholarship; and the discipline as a whole lacks the heady growth of the 1960s and early 1970s. To overcome the first problem a number of new editions, or entirely new works, have been commissioned – some have already appeared. To deal with the second, the aim remains to publish up-to-date introductions to important areas of debate. If the series can demonstrate to students and their teachers the importance of the discipline of economic and social history and excite its further study, it will continue the task so ably begun by its first two editors.

The Queen's University of Belfast L. A. CLARKSON
General Editor

1 Introduction

The history of the recent past, even that within living memory, is subject to sudden changes in perception. Some of the reasons for this are obvious – official records are opened, memoirs are written, documents are found. Less obviously, historians try to grapple with a period which has directly shaped the present. As Britain entered on a new period of rising unemployment and calls for government retrenchment in the 1970s, it was tempting to make comparisons with the 1930s. This is not necessarily to say that historians offer merely a crude reflection of their own times, but that when new problems arise, old problems appear in a different light. In both periods, social policy seemed to be closely related to the government's handling of an economic crisis, and changes in the fortunes of the Welfare State naturally provoked new questions about the past. In the prosperous 1960s, historians were severely critical of interwar policies: in the uncertain 1980s these policies seemed more understandable, even inevitable.

Social policy is a loose term, which might include anything from divorce laws to drinking hours. For the purposes of this book it is defined in a very basic way as the state's investment in support of the material welfare of the people, either through the maintenance of incomes or provision of services such as health care and housing. Moral and cultural investment, such as state education, are also important in a nation's economic life, but the arguments which influence such policies are rather different, and will be considered in less detail here.

The opening of official records, sometimes received with uncritical enthusiasm [11], has encouraged many new studies. Unemployment tends to attract most attention, but there has also been much reassessment of health, housing, and poverty in general. Because of the wide range of issues, discussion of social policy tends to be fragmented. Unlike some other contentious historical questions, the debate does not resemble a football match between two reasonably orderly teams, but one where the play on the field is secondary to the numerous fights breaking out in the stands.

Although different areas of policy require separate treatment, they are linked both by the question of finance and by more general arguments about social inequalities. After 1919, unemployment was the issue which permeated most aspects of policy. Its heavy cost affected the proportion of national expenditure which could be devoted to other social services and, at the same time, it was said to make other social problems worse. Administrators do not always accept that unemployment exacerbates other social conditions such as ill-health, but both contemporaries and historians have tried to see whether a relationship existed.

Few would claim that either the economic or the social policies of interwar governments were dynamic; rather, the debate concerns their adequacy in difficult circumstances. Increasingly, the debate has focused on a question with present-day significance: whether the interwar years demonstrate that a solid foundation for social welfare can be laid even in depression, or whether effective social policy is a luxury which only a buoyant economy can afford.

2   Agents of Policy

(i) MOTIVATION AND THE 'WELFARE CONSENSUS'

Interpretations of the motives for social policy at any time expose
fundamental differences of view, as shown in Hay's survey of the
Liberal welfare reforms written for this series [48]. He summarises
two major interpretations of social policy: the local and the
international. Local explanations describe how policy arises out of
specific political situations, such as the rise of New Liberalism in
Britain before 1914. Policy may be decided through the accommo-
dations between political elites or it may be a panicky response to
sudden demands from potentially dangerous sections of the
population. The history of social policy lends itself to intricate
political analysis, and several accounts, notably those of Gilbert,
Skidelsky and Morgan, reveal the complexity of such negotiations in
the interwar years [40; 89; 75].

Hay himself stresses the second, or international aspect of social
policy: that the growth of and motives for new welfare systems were
common to many developed countries in the late nineteenth
century. In particular, fear of falling behind in the economic or
military race made governments adopt social policy as an engine of
national efficiency. Such an explanation may assume that governments act quite autonomously: alternatively, governments in industrial society might be seen as bowing to inexorable pressure from
the rise of new social forces, particularly the labour movement. New
types of social policy were therefore the 'response of capitalist
societies to the experience of economic growth' [48, 62]. During the
war and the interwar years the developed world greatly increased its
spending on social welfare [64], and many countries had to respond
to high levels of unemployment. International comparisons, which
have usually been more attractive to welfare economists than to
historians, are outlined by Marshall and Thane [66; 96].

Histories of social policy might also be fitted into 'pluralist' and
'elitist' models. The pluralist model sees social policy as an outcome

11

of conflict between classes and interest groups, in which consensus has to be reached to ensure social peace. The conflict may include the threat of force, but it can also result from democratic debate or backstage negotiations. The elitist model sees policy as determined in the interests of the economically dominant classes, usually well represented in the bureaucracy, who will ensure that debates on social policy take place within narrow limits. Webb suggests that social policy in Britain is usually a compromise between these two positions, in that pressure from outside may lead to policy changes, but those in authority will determine the shape and extent of change [43, *Ch. 8*].

This is a crude summary of refined arguments, and it would be needlessly offensive to the historians whose work is the subject of this essay, to suggest that they can be divided rigidly into ideological camps. On the contrary, the history of social policy often demonstrates a very British distaste for overt theory, and is apt to subside into a soporific narrative of legislation. There may be good reasons for this: defenders of the pragmatic approach argue that the few attempts to base social policy on an openly stated theory of social relationships have been highly unpopular, for example the 1834 Poor Law. Nevertheless, we should consider the views which underpin some of the most widely read histories, and how the historiography of interwar policy has changed with the times.

Maurice Bruce in *The Coming of the Welfare State* (1961) leaned towards a pluralist model, which saw modern social policy as the result of centuries of 'struggle for social justice' [17, 7]. He emphasised that the outcome of this struggle had not been planned, and that the Welfare State had finally emerged from an expanding economy and full employment rather than redistribution of income. Like many writers on social policy, Bruce was very interested in the rise of state responsibility (collectivism), and whether it had undermined individual effort. His belief in continuing progress towards social consensus led him to an optimistic conclusion [17, *333*].

In this view, as in the influential work of T. H. Marshall (1965), twentieth-century policy had two heroic moments: the Liberal Welfare Reforms of 1906–14, and the Labour legislation of 1945–50. The period between was by no means lacking in achievement, but it was less inspiring. The peaks were crowned with the work of visionaries, planners and energetic politicians – Lloyd George,

Churchill, the Webbs, Beveridge, Bevan. The interwar years were more prosaic, for government accepted the responsibilities which it had acquired before 1914, but was content to build on them rather than to innovate. Insurance was extended but the Poor Law remained; local government was more closely tied to central policy, but still took very independent decisions; more public hospitals were built, but the greatest hospitals were still run by charity. All policy had to adjust to sudden economic crisis and the stagnation of Britain's staple industries until the late 1930s. Governments were not inactive, but policy was inadequate against the 'overwhelming social despair of the inter-war years' [17, *328*].

Gilbert's major study offered an even more positive view of the interwar consensus. By 1939: 'the British State had committed itself to the maintenance of all its citizens according to need as a matter of right without any concurrent political disability' [40, *308*]. The policy of the interwar years arose less from the search for social justice than from the pressures of a wider electorate, the growth of the Labour Party and, above all, the need to prevent unrest from 'society's most dangerous and volatile element, the unemployed adult male' [40, *viii*]. Gilbert's work indicates how the pluralist and elitist theories may be reconciled, for although he accepts the importance of labour protest and pressure groups as agents of policy, he also shows how the essential details of policy are decided by elites in ministerial corridors.

Other historians have found less consensus in the interwar years. In 1973 Fraser, while giving credit for achievement, saw policy as pragmatic, piecemeal and limited, requiring the cataclysm of war to produce the impetus for change. By the time of his second edition in 1984, he was arguing that even the post-1945 consensus was beginning to crumble [36, *251*]. Thane's interpretation is also closely related to the problems of the 1980s: like Gilbert she accepts that consensus arose less from the search for social justice than from the need for political accommodation, but she stresses the importance of the quest for economic stability, and especially that social policy had to fit into contemporary theories of the 'efficient use of resources' [96, *300*]. Peden (1985) also shows that economic policy dominated in the 1930s, since government priorities lay with the restraint of public expenditure, and so economic and financial theories were used to justify government inaction in social policy [80, *82, 233–4*].

Post-war histories of the origins of the Welfare State have tended to move away from idealism as an explanation for social policy, and have stressed political accommodation or economic determinism instead. But comparisons with their own times have never been far from the surface.

(ii) THE EXTENT OF INTERVENTION

An important measure of government commitment to social policy is expenditure. Although Victorian governments had taken much interest in social policy, new services had been paid for mainly from local rates and administered by local government. Lloyd George's welfare reforms, financed partly from national taxation, ensured that social policy in the twentieth century would be tied to the economic policy of the state. Between 1918 and 1938, government expenditure on the social services rose considerably, though not as dramatically as after the Second World War, and attempts at retrenchment in 1922 and 1931 had only a temporary effect (see columns 1 and 3 in Table 1). The social services also absorbed higher proportions of expenditure every year until rearmament began in the late 1930s (column 2).

The figures also show the great leap between pre-war and post-war commitments after both wars. The sudden surge in social spending between 1918 and 1921 was very noticeable. This was partly because the government had to raise pensions to keep up with inflation [40, *239*], while a new burden was created by war pensions and then by the onset of unemployment in 1921. Other post-war programmes, particularly in housing, committed government both to immediate expense and to long-term subsidies [78, *205*]. Yet even in the trough of the depression of the early 1930s spending on social services rose, and the percentage of GNP devoted to them increased (column 4). Peden argues that the 'onward march' of social services continued in spite of government economies and balanced budgets [80, *112*].

The significance of these statistics is debatable. The leap in government expenditure just after the war is undoubted, but the proportion of GNP devoted to social policy in the two succeeding decades is much less remarkable. The total expenditure of British governments in relation to GNP was growing much more slowly

Table 1   Local and Central Government Expenditure on Social Services in the
UK 1913–1951

Year	(1) Total expenditure (current prices) £m	(2) % of total gvt expenditure	(3) £ per head of population	(4) as % of GNP	(5) Local gvt expenditure on social services[a] as % of total gvt expenditure
1913	100.8	33.0	2.2	4.1	64
1915	93.4	9.7	2.0	3.4	71
1917	127.8	8.4	2.7	3.3	52
1918	114.3	4.7	2.4	2.4	59
1920	411.8	25.9	9.4	6.8	35
1921	490.7	34.3	11.1	10.1	37
1922	423.2	35.9	9.5	10.0	41
1923	358.7	35.0	8.0	8.5	43
1924	365.0	35.5	8.1	8.4	43
1925	389.3	36.3	8.6	8.8	44
1926	424.4	38.4	9.4	9.9	46
1927	436.0	39.4	9.6	9.5	45
1928	434.3	39.7	9.5	9.6	43
1929	438.0	39.6	9.6	9.5	43
1930	484.7	42.3	10.6	11.1	40
1931	516.8	44.0	11.2	12.7	38
1932	511.1	44.9	11.0	12.9	37
1933	497.2	46.6	10.7	12.0	38
1934	498.3	47.0	10.7	11.5	40
1935	519.2	46.5	11.1	11.3	41
1936	532.7	44.9	11.3	11.1	43
1937	554.4	42.5	11.7	10.9	44
1938	596.3	37.6	12.5	11.3	44
1950	2,094	46.1	41.7	18.0	23
1951	2,234	42.9	44.4	17.5	25

[a]Excludes housing
Source: [78, 184–91]

than in other developed countries, especially in the 1930s [64, 57].
The increase also seems less if allowances are made for the effects of
unemployment: Peacock and Wiseman noted that higher expenditure between the wars was related to high unemployment, and did

not necessarily reflect a long-term commitment. The proportion of GNP devoted to the social services rose quite sharply between 1918 and 1922 and again between 1929 and 1933, but declined when unemployment diminished [78, *50*]. Social expenditure in the interwar years was thus heavily committed to meeting an emergency which could not be ignored without political consequences: as Peden's own figures show, other social services, particularly education and health, fared much less well [80, *76, 111*]. These, being left largely to local option, showed great regional variations. By comparison, a much higher amount of GNP was allocated to the social services in the early 1950s, at a time of virtually full employment.

More fundamental changes occurred in the balance of expenditure between central and local government (column 5). Central responsibility for pensions and health insurance was greatly extended in 1925, when old age pensions changed from a non-contributory to a contributory basis, and could therefore be offered to many more people. Widows' and orphans' pensions were also introduced, so that many people who would in the past have been entitled only to local Poor Law relief, could now make claims on national taxation. But government responsibility for the unemployed, undertaken as the soldiers returned from the trenches, was the most significant and expensive innovation.

Nevertheless, local government was still important in social policy. The Victorian practice of allowing local authorities to decide whether or not to take up government subsidies persisted, especially in housing and education, where costs were divided between local and central authority. Local authorities kept their responsibility for many services, especially public health. They could obtain government aid for large capital projects such as hospitals, but took their own decisions on what kind of service to offer, above a basic obligation to prevent the spread of infection. Local, not national, government was responsible for the bulk of capital investment of public funds [70, *46*].

In addition, local authorities still took care of everyone not covered by national insurance. For example, most of the unemployed could claim state benefits, but a sizeable minority who were refused benefit had no other choice than poor relief. The effect of government intervention was not to reduce but to supplement the amount spent by local authorities on social services. Since the

16

depression was much more severe in some regions than in others, it put a heavy burden on local as well as national finances [85, *160*]. Poor relief, which had been about a fifth of local current expenditure in 1920, took up almost a quarter of a much larger budget in 1933, even though central government bore most of the cost of the unemployed [78, *116–17*].

In Scotland, an important group gained new access to public relief. The Scottish Poor Law was more inflexible than the English, and had denied able-bodied people any legal right to relief – in England, outdoor labour or the workhouse could be used as a test of destitution. Scottish local authorities had previously coped with emergencies in the labour market by raising charitable donations. High levels of unemployment in the stagnating heavy industries after the war hit Scotland particularly hard, and the Scottish Poor Law was inadequate to deal with such an emergency; from 1921 it was regularly suspended to allow relief to the able-bodied. State doles and local poor relief were therefore available to a group which previously would have relied largely on charity [56].

After the First World War, income tax, rather than regressive indirect taxation, provided the larger share of government income. Unlike the post-1945 Welfare State, most personal social services were means tested: national insurance was available only to low-wage earners, public hospitals charged fees to higher earners, and so on. By 1939 about 18 separate means tests were in operation [26, *136*]. It might therefore be argued that welfare spending in the interwar period had a more important effect in redistributing income in favour of the working classes than in either of the periods encircling it. Contemporary investigation of this subject was undertaken by Barna, who concluded that working-class income in 1937 had been increased by between 8 and 14 per cent through social expenditure, mainly at the expense of those earning more than £2,000 p.a. He added, however, that this was not very remarkable in view of the numbers of unemployed: still 1.5 million in 1937. If their numbers had been reduced by a third, the amount saved in transfer payments to them would have virtually wiped out the effects of redistribution [6, *232–3*].

When considering the various estimates of government expenditure and its effects in the interwar period, the implications of Barna's argument should be remembered. The unemployed required their whole income to be provided through transfer payments, even though they were capable of maintaining themselves. The amount of GNP which the state devoted to uninsured benefits, around 2.0 per cent in 1931 [41, *254*], may have diverted finances from other groups. Since the unemployed also put pressure on other services such as health care and free school meals, local authorities may have worried more about meeting the emergency demands on the social services than about ways of extending their coverage or improving their quality.

(iii) THE MAKERS OF POLICY

Who made social policy in this period? Possible participants include politicians, bureaucrats and organised pressure groups, including the Labour movement. Gilbert stresses the private nature of much policy-making at this time, except for rare occasions when social questions suddenly dominated Parliament, as when the Labour government was split in 1931 by its decision to cut unemployment benefits [40, *307*]. Ministers were either inactive or, like Christopher Addison, not in office long enough to implement their wishes. The only exception was Neville Chamberlain, an unusually competent Minister of Health, whose long spell in that office, combined with his enthusiasm for bureaucratic detail, enabled him to extend national insurance and reform local government.

It would be misleading, however, to assume that this period lacked public debate on social policy, for social affairs generated an enormous literature, from the essays of Orwell and Priestley to the statistical surveys of Rowntree and Boyd Orr. Yet the very growth of bureaucratic social administration tended to divert the minds of politicians away from fundamentals and down to the daily details which occupied government departments. Social policy did not significantly divide Labour from Conservative governments, with the possible exception of Wheatley's vigorous housing policy of 1924. Political arguments were usually over details such as the level of the dole, and even the great split of 1931 was over the preservation of the *status quo* rather than innovation in policy [89, *61*]. Historians of the Labour Party are often pained by its financial conservatism, which Churchill encapsulated in his reminiscence of the Labour Chancellor: 'The Treasury mind and the Snowden mind embraced each other with the fervour of two long-separated kindred lizards' [89, *86*]. The Treasury, however, was less like a lizard than a boa-constrictor, whose embrace Churchill himself had not escaped when he was Chancellor.

In those years when there were few forceful politicians, and the forceful ones like Chamberlain had orthodox opinions on finance, the bureaucracy was well placed to influence policy. The higher civil service was probably at the peak of its influence in the interwar years [81, *210*]. The administrative machinery was enormously enlarged and strengthened during the war, as the government was forced to take charge of essential production and the labour market. New bureaucracies emerged, notably the Ministry of Labour and the Ministry of Health, while the civil service as a whole doubled in size between 1913 and 1939 [60, *291*].

During the war and immediate post-war years welfare ministers had low status in the Cabinet, and led weak ministries, which were regarded 'either as a transitional step to higher office or as a graveyard where a dying career could be quietly buried' [40, *307*]. Addison, who was Minister successively for Reconstruction and Health found that his progressive views were constantly thwarted both by his ministerial colleagues and by forces within the civil service [76, *Chs 3–5*]. The Ministry of Reconstruction, which should have been the crucible for post-war renewal, had no authority and was resented by other ministries. The Ministry of Health was not the vital force which Addison had intended, but had also to operate the Poor Law with its stubborn and old-fashioned administrators. Lowe, in an early essay on the Ministry of Labour, also claimed that the administrative weakness of the civil service inhibited social policy. The Ministry's staff were of lower calibre than in the pre-war Board of Trade, and it wasted energy in futile battles with other government departments [58, *436*].

Beloff defended the civil service, claiming with justice that its operations had not been thoroughly examined [81, *210*]. Lowe also had second thoughts on bureaucratic ineptitude, and argued that the civil service was slowly learning to live in a more democratic world: the Ministry of Labour, for example, had to take much more account of the attitudes of both employers and trade unions than had the paternalistic pre-war bureaucracies [60, *298–300*]. Lowe's own study of the Ministry of Labour helped to fill a considerable gap in the history of the bureaucracy, with Lowe arguing for an 'incrementalist' interpretation of social policy: the pressures of a

19

newly democratic state were met not by dramatic shifts of policy, but by a continual series of small-scale adjustments [61].

There was once little disagreement that Treasury control was the main cause of inaction in government departments. The Treasury's authority grew during and after the war: at first the new 'mushroom ministries' successfully demanded new funds for the war effort, but in 1919 the Treasury reasserted its power over public expenditure and forced economies, backed by 'the support of most of the vocal public' [18, *100*]. With a more modern establishment, it had even greater control over the size of other government departments and the appointment of senior civil servants, a rule 'that made it unwise for any ambitious civil servant ever to fall foul of the Treasury' [58, *428*]. Although the Treasury claimed that politicians, not civil servants, were responsible for formulating policy, its financial power made it the ultimate arbiter of all policy, and so the 'Treasury view' on expenditure was of enormous importance. As will be seen, this has led several historians to cast the Treasury in the role of the Demon King during the interwar years [107; 45]. A revisionist interpretation suggests that the Treasury did not have to impose its will on reluctant colleagues: greater mobility between government departments led to a cosy homogeneity of opinion in the civil service, in which the search for economies was much encouraged [22, *109*].

In order to formulate policy, government needs adequate information. Marshall asserted that the interwar period revealed a more scientific approach to social policy: 'Before the first war social reform was a political adventure run by enthusiastic amateurs; in the inter-war years social administration became a science practised by professionals' [66, *61*]. He had in mind the practical methods of Neville Chamberlain or the statistical methods used by interwar researchers, compared with the haphazard strategies of Asquith's government. Yet this 'scientific' approach should not be exaggerated. Before 1914, even the most efficient government departments tended to compile statistics to prove subjective points, and interwar statistics are by no means innocent of the same intention.

Government statistics had large gaps. No official estimate of GNP was made until the Second World War, hence spending on social and other services tended to be quoted as a gross amount, not related to the nation's capacity to pay for them. The statistics of unemployment are another trap, since the Ministry of Labour collected seemingly authoritative figures supplied by the labour exchanges, rather than the limited information available from a few trade unions before the war. By one reckoning, unemployment statistics overestimate the rate of unemployment in the population because they count only insured workers, thus leaving out large uninsured groups with low unemployment, such as agricultural labourers [41, *ch. 5*]. By another reckoning the figures ignore unemployment among other groups such as those under 16, who are not entitled to claim benefit [37, *38–40*]. Several administrative changes in the definition of unemployment produced statistical hiccoughs. In the early 1920s, the Treasury also undermined the efficiency of the Statistics Department of the Ministry of Labour by reducing its manpower [61: *193*].

Similar criticisms apply to the Ministry of Health's statistics, since the Ministry was traditionally more interested in mortality than in morbidity; its statistics therefore relate to deaths and infectious disease rather than sickness generally [100, *118*]. Even though many doctors were now working in the panel service of the national insurance scheme, their records were not used for any statistical purpose [23, *178*]. Historians continue to fall back on rather limited unofficial studies of health and poverty, such as Boyd Orr's work on nutrition, or the Pilgrim Trust's study of the unemployed.

Social policy was a natural target for the action of pressure groups, which even before 1914 had reached a high degree of sophistication in British political life. Some, such as the TUC and the National Confederation of Employers' Organisations (NCEO), lobbied over social policy whenever it seemed to affect class interests. Their most direct concern in this period was the extent and finance of national insurance, since both worker and employer contributed to the scheme. The building trade was affected by the government's housing policies, and the insurance companies by health policies, since they had a large stake in national health insurance. Professional associations also held views on policy, but the most important by far was the British Medical Association, whose influence had been greatly strengthened after 1911 when national insurance brought many doctors into a financial relationship with the state. Other pressure groups were organised with one particular aim, such as Eleanor Rathbone's Family Endowment Society, which campaigned for family allowances, or Marie Stopes's Society for Constructive Birth Control and Racial Progress.

The *ad hoc* societies will appear in the discussion of particular policies, but the influence of class interests has inevitably aroused controversy. Employers have received less attention than the labour movement. Hay, who had studied the role of employers' organisations in social policy before 1914, felt that the depression had altered their attitudes. Previously they had often approved certain types of social insurance as a means of control and greater industrial efficiency, but the weakness of British industry between the wars made them resist the extra costs of extending national insurance [49, 6]. Hence the NCEO argued in 1926 'there is a definite limit to the amount of money which any country can afford to spend in the providing of social services . . . that limit has in Great Britain already been largely exceeded' [49, *46*].

Other studies reveal that, particularly from the late 1920s, the employers' own welfare plans proliferated, mainly to forestall state intervention. Employers were largely successful in persuading the government to accept voluntary arrangements for health and welfare in the workplace, but these schemes were more extensive in the new industries in the south, where it was necessary to attract skilled workers. Employers' policies thus exacerbated the north-south division in social welfare [54]. Hannah's study of occupational schemes accepts, like Hay, that employers often favoured welfare schemes to strengthen the existing social order; but finds a more positive attitude towards workers' pensions in the interwar period. Some of the larger employers in the successful industries, such as Courtaulds and Austin, supported improvements in the state pension system. Before the war, large-scale firms had begun to establish their own pension schemes for their workers, and changes in the tax law in 1921 encouraged this further. Private-sector pensions expanded in spite of the depression [46, *18-20, 38*].

The influence of the Labour movement on social policy has been much discussed. The Labour Party had finally become a serious force in politics, and all politicians had at least to consider the electoral implications of social policy. The electorate was much enlarged in 1918, and people receiving Poor Law relief or other state subsidies were able to vote. This directly affected local politics. Yet the Labour movement was deeply divided, and those within it who threatened to undermine conventional social administration were not welcomed by the leadership. George Lansbury and the unruly councillors of Poplar embarrassed the Labour leaders of the

LCC [15, *132*]; the radicals in the National Unemployed Workers' Movement, founded in 1921, had little support from the TUC [92, *Ch. 9*]; Oswald Mosley's efforts to promote Continental views on public works to create jobs had a dusty response from the Parliamentary party [107, *132*]. Criticism of the Labour leadership usually refers to their urge to appear respectable to the voters, or the growth of a self-regarding bureaucracy in the trade unions [90, *Ch. 8*]. The Labour Party was uncertain whether, in order to prevent social distress, it should try to shore up the capitalist system, or stand back and wait for its gradual but inevitable demise. The radicals, on the other hand, have been seen by many from the Webbs onwards as Utopian and feckless [99, *905*].

Neither were the trade unions in a position to provide effective leadership for much of the period, though their weakness can be exaggerated. Unemployment threatens the size and power of unions: union membership, which had been at a peak during the war, fell off rapidly thereafter, especially after 1926. As one dispirited member of the unemployed told H. L. Beales in 1934: 'The trade unions have never been any good since the General Strike, and nobody else bothers about us.'[1] Nevertheless, the power of the unions was far from broken, and employers wished to avoid further confrontation. In spite of unemployment, real wages rose in the 1930s. Rather, the unions tended to avoid entanglement in social policy: they were suspicious of family allowances because these might be used to undercut wages [63, *142*] and, apart from demanding that unemployment benefits be kept at a decent level, their most positive demand over unemployment was that it be reduced by raising the school-leaving age and imposing the 40-hour week. Pollard has argued that Bevin and other union leaders were being converted to Keynes rather than Marx during the interwar crisis. They had already developed an interest in public works programmes which the New Deal confirmed, but this was not in the forefront of their agenda in the 1930s [84, *161*].

The influence of the Labour movement in social policy therefore focuses on the threat of unofficial protest. Policy based on the threat of violence has been discerned in wartime rent controls [68, *Ch. 3*], the hasty introduction of uninsured unemployment benefits in 1918 [40, *59*], and in the Coalition government's housing plans [93; 94]. Tighter administration of benefits in the 1920s and the increasingly parsimonious attitude to housing might conversely be seen as a sign that governments were less troubled by such fears, especially after the fiasco of the General Strike. Benefits could be reduced and the means test imposed in 1931 without arousing more than small-scale and sporadic protest. Yet in 1935 the National government altered its programme for central control of unemployment benefit after popular demonstrations [73]. Even when government was not confronted by the threat of direct action, it had to take into account the *possibility* of such action: this prevented, for example, any thoroughgoing effort to revive the Poor Law after the war, even though sections of the Ministry of Health would have strongly favoured this [71; 28, *94*].

The question of whether the unemployed seriously threatened social order is obviously of current interest. Gilbert sees the potential for violence as one of the main themes linking interwar social policy. Evidence comes from the alarmist reports which were passed to the Coalition government by Sir Basil Thomson, head of the Directorate of Intelligence. Discounting Thomson's discovery of Bolshevik activities in all sections of the labour movement in the early months of 1919, Gilbert nevertheless accepts that there was widespread and genuine grievance among the working class in which fear of unemployment and the loss of status among skilled workers had a part [40, *26–9*]. From this time onwards, the unemployed were a potentially dangerous force which government could not ignore.

Others have disputed whether the unemployed were ever seen as a threat. Even if the government were alarmed into handing out indiscriminate doles to the unemployed between 1918 and 1921, this fear was short-lived, for the administration of benefit was rapidly tightened, and the process of claiming it became more humiliating [31]. In any case, the Ministry of Labour received Thomson's reports sceptically [75, *53*]. Extremist parties, either Communist or Fascist, made little impact in the 1930s in spite of unemployment [92, *123*]. Stevenson claims that the 1935 campaign against the new scales of unemployment benefit succeeded not because of the threat of violence, but because the issue had finally roused the TUC and other official labour organisations in support of the unemployed [81, *162*], and because an election was imminent [91, *208*]. Miller argues that the Labour organisations themselves acted only after violent demonstrations in Wales and Scotland took them by surprise [73, *330–1*], but in any case policy was temporarily

24

deflected rather than altered.

Stevenson argues that the unemployed did not seriously threaten social order because the short-term unemployed still hoped for work, while the long-term unemployed lapsed into a fatalism in which politics seemed irrelevant [92, *160*]. Orwell made much the same comment in 1937 regarding the cheapness of working-class pleasures:

> It is quite likely that fish-and-chips, art-silk stockings, tinned salmon, cut-price chocolate (five two-ounce bars for sixpence), the movies, the radio, strong tea and the Football Pools have between them averted revolution.[2]

It is not really crucial for the historian of social policy to debate the precise shade of vermilion of Red Clydeside or the success of the National Unemployed Workers' Movement (NUWM) in rousing working-class support. For even if the threat of violence was never very serious, interwar governments could not ignore it. The police and other intelligence agencies were constantly looking out for 'Bolshevik' elements in disobedient local councils, in the General Strike, and in any other movements of protest. Police and local government officers were encouraged to make life as difficult as possible for hunger marches which were organised by the NUWM, and prison became a familiar experience for NUWM leaders like Wal Hannington. If the threat of violence did not cause great alarm, it nevertheless encouraged a cautious approach, based on the need to maintain some kind of working relationship with the trade unions. During the war, government had looked towards the unions to help safeguard industrial production and had come to realise that it was not the unions but the unofficial labour organisations which were the greater threat. Even in the years from 1919 to 1926, when industrial strife in Britain reached its height, government continued to see the unions as a bulwark against more militant agitators [75, *75*]. Ultimately, the labour movement was neither strong nor coherent enough to force government into new ways of thinking, but it defined what government could *not* do.

3 The First World War and After

In order to see some of these forces in action, it is instructive to follow the course of social policy during the war and Lloyd George's Coalition government of 1918–22. During the war, the government had hesitantly subjected the economy to unprecedented controls, most of which were scrapped soon after the war's end. Social policy appeared to follow a similar pattern, with an outburst of national fervour for reform dissipating amidst post-war crisis and retrenchment. Marwick concluded that political institutions had failed to keep pace with the social change generated by war [67, *334*]; Milward that social change was not as significant as economic change [74, *26*]. This period illustrates the interlocking political, social and economic factors which shape social policy, and raises the question of whether the war produced more than temporary innovations in social welfare.

Andrzejewski's theory of the 'military participation ratio', maintains that as modern war becomes larger in scale, so it needs the efforts of larger sections of the population: war therefore encourages social equality and sharing of benefits [4]. His theory has provoked many attacks, including those of Milward [74] and Abrams [2] who have not found that the First World War produced much social levelling or increased interest in social welfare. Nevertheless, continual references to the theory imply that it is too suggestive to be ignored, especially in the more cautious form put forward by Titmuss [97, *86*]: that although the social effects of modern warfare are not predictable, war increases public demand for welfare and equality, and encourages greater government responsibility. At a very simple level, the First World War stimulated government concern with national efficiency in two areas: maximising output in the war industries and preserving the national stock by protecting the health of mothers and children.

Factory Acts which limited working hours were suspended, for the factories needed the labour of women and young people. In 1915 the Ministry of Munitions, having acquired wider powers over industry, rapidly directed its attention towards the welfare of workers in the war industries; its chief concerns were absenteeism, overwork (since fatigue led to diminished efficiency), and ill-health. Employers had a tax incentive to promote factory welfare for they could claim against the costs of works canteens, rest rooms and the wages of welfare supervisors. The government encouraged medical research, particularly into the effects of fatigue on productivity, and investigated the benefits of scientific management through 'time and motion' studies.

Much of this intervention was short-lived, as controls were abandoned after the war and women left the factories. The government continued to sponsor the Medical Research Council and the Industrial Health Research Board, but employers had no obligation to continue their welfare measures. This might be seen as yet another example of welfare gestures abandoned in peacetime, but the workers themselves often resented such intervention. Welfare supervisors intruded into workers' personal lives and were suspected of undermining the influence of the trade unions [104].

Phillips and Whiteside apply similar arguments to the effects of war on the casual labour market. Edwardian reformers had taken much interest in decasualisation, particularly on the docks, since casual labour was thought not only to cause poverty, but also to demoralise the workman. Government controls over labour mobility effectively decasualised many workers during the war, but were promptly abandoned in peacetime. These controls had also been unpopular with both employers and workmen, since they reduced the amounts earned by the most successful dockers, while attacking the personal freedom which was one of the few advantages of a docker's life [82, Ch. 4]. Attempts to fix minimum wages in traditionally low-paid occupations gained some momentum during the war, but met a similar fate in 1921 [59].

The health of mothers and infants was a subject which aroused great emotion during the war, as indicated in the well-publicised argument that high infant mortality made it more dangerous to be a baby than a soldier. In fact infant mortality, which had already begun to decline at the beginning of the twentieth century, continued to fall sharply during the war, especially amongst babies who had survived the perilous first month of life [108]. The government encouraged local authorities to improve their services to mothers and babies, and would pay half the cost towards ante-natal and child-care clinics, home visitors, hospital treatment, and food for necessitous mothers and children. But local authorities reacted in different ways, while some medical officers believed firmly that infant mortality was due to the bad habits of the working classes. The BMA also tried to discourage GPs from taking part in clinics because they might undermine general practice [111, *203*]. Nevertheless, clinics and health visitors proliferated, though it was not until 1918 that the Maternity and Child Welfare Act obliged local authorities to set up committees to deal with the subject – and even then they were not compelled to provide specific services [57, *34*].

Medical care and advice may have aided the survival of newborn infants, but better nutrition of mothers and children had more far-reaching effects [108, *499*]. Wage increases, which barely kept up with rising prices for food and rent, probably had less effect on nutrition than did the levelling upwards of wages in less skilled occupations, virtual elimination of unemployment and the oppor-tunity for more members of the family to work. Government measures to ration milk in 1917 may also have improved family diets. Yet neither policy nor better nutrition benefited the elderly, whose death rate actually rose during the war. Fit elderly people could often find employment during the war: the less able were dependent on incomes from pensions or poor relief, which were eroded by inflation. Demands for national efficiency diverted social policy away from the elderly, who before 1914 had received much attention from reformers, but who were now removed from hospitals and institutions to make way for the wounded [27, *92*]. Changes in mortality rates cannot be attributed to precise causes, and it is difficult to weigh the effects of government policy against other factors, but rising incomes certainly had a more widespread effect than patchy local provision of health services.

Civilian health improved even though 14,000 doctors had been diverted to military service during the war, and Winter concludes the lack of medical attention did not prevent an increase in the nation's life expectancy [111, *186–7*]. The most positive measures were in the treatment of tuberculosis and venereal disease, which both spread more rapidly in wartime conditions and threatened the efficiency of troops and workers. New drugs made a cure for VD possible, and although there was no remedy for TB, it could be contained by isolating sufferers. The government made free treatment for tuberculosis available to insured workers, and then to the whole population in 1921. Public opinion still prevented simple prophylactics against VD from being openly given to the troops, but the government attempted to prevent infection of the civilian population by an Act of 1917 whch permitted free and confidential treatment in local authority clinics.

In one important area the government was impelled to act less through its own sense of the emergency than by pressure from below. Reluctance to interfere with the market in the early years of the war extended to such basic matters as food and rent. Yet the workers who flocked into the war industries put enormous pressure on local housing. In some smaller towns, such as Rosyth, the government provided houses or hostels, but not in large cities like Glasgow, even though pre-war housing conditions had been poor, and private housebuilding had virtually ended after war broke out. For many workers in the affected cities, rising rents effectively cancelled out any gains from improved wages.

In 1915, rent strikes began in a number of cities, but they were mainly associated with Clydeside, where the government was already troubled by unrest in the war industries. This has usually been described as a wartime emergency [67, *135*], but more recently Melling has related it to long-standing and complicated struggles over housing on the Clyde. In 1915 the employers did not discourage the rent protest because they recognised that high rents put pressure on wages; they hoped that government intervention might reduce their own responsibilities [68, *148*]. The government dealt harshly with the leaders of industrial unrest on Clydeside, but the women who pelted rent collectors with rotten fish or protected their neighbours from eviction could not easily be branded as traitors to the war effort, especially as some of them were the wives of men at the front. The government may have been as concerned with the effect of evictions on the morale of troops as with the possible disruption of the war industries.

The Rent and Mortgage interest (War Restrictions) Act of 1915, which controlled the level of working-class rents, was the first major incursion of government into the housing market. Combined with the rise in interest rates and the high cost of building after the war, it

29

discouraged private investment in houses for rent. Rent controls could not be given up immediately after the war because the housing shortage and high cost of building would have pushed up rents to unacceptable levels, and so the state was forced to intervene. Yet even before the war, new land taxes had made rents a less safe speculative investment, and government had begun to investigate housing conditions; Daunton argues, however, that intervention in favour of council housing was unlikely without the pressure of emergency, since pre-war housing reformers had concentrated chiefly on philanthropy and land tax reforms. Lacking sufficient political influence, 'private landlords and mortgagees were one of the few sectors of property sacrificed by the government during the war' [29, *8*].

(ii) THE FAILURE OF RECONSTRUCTION

Wartime welfare measures before 1917 were therefore either modest in scale or unplanned. The main test of Andrzjewski's thesis applies to the plans for reconstruction devised from 1917 onwards by the Ministry of Reconstruction and other official committees. The failure of the Coalition government to press on with reconstruction is all the more noticeable because the plans themselves were so far ranging: they included the virtual abolition of the Poor Law; a massive extension and improvement of state education; industrial tribunals of workers and employers to arbitrate on wages and other matters; a Ministry of Health which should co-ordinate and expand the country's health services; unemployment insurance for all workers; extended pension schemes; and finally, as the war ended, Lloyd George's own promise of homes for heroes. Some of these proposals, such as universal insurance and the abolition of the Poor Law, sank before the war ended; others, including housing and education, survived, but became the emaciated victims of post-war economies.

At the time, many people wanted to hang the Kaiser; subsequently there has been more interest in hanging the effigies of those responsible for retrenchment, but the culprits have been difficult to identify. Historians have tended to produce political, economic or administrative reasons for the failure of reform, according to their particular expertise, though of course these explanations are not necessarily contradictory.

Two major contemporary explanations long held the field, mainly because they satisfyingly represented the division in political opinion. On one hand, there was Lloyd George's own explanation which naturally blamed factors outside his control: that the economy had 'run mad', making economies inevitable [77, *129ff*]. On the other hand, Keynes's famous description in *The Economic Consequences of the Peace* suited those who were looking for signs of political betrayal: the Coalition government had been taken over by 'hard-faced men who looked as if they had done very well out of the war', and had put reform on the bonfire together with most of the other wartime economic controls.

Dissatisfaction with these explanations was voiced by Abrams [2], who argued that, for two reasons, the impetus for reform was slackening even before the slump or before the Coalition Parliament had met. Firstly, many politicians interpreted 'reconstruction' literally as a return to pre-war values. The war had not caused any real social levelling or shaken the government's faith in the free market: hence even those like Addison who were strongly committed to reform were reluctant to maintain government controls over the economy. Secondly, the machinery of government had not been overhauled enough to permit central direction for reconstruction, and venomous intrigues broke out between the various ministers and their civil servants.

Abrams' timing of the loss of reforming initiative has been questioned, since the Coalition government was apparently pushing ahead with its programme for housing and education well into 1920 [75, *95*]: but his criticism of the administrative framework is often supported. The new ministries were inadequate to carry the burden of reconstruction. The Ministry of Labour, for example, did not lack reforming zeal, but was not bold enough to challenge Treasury orthodoxy on financial matters and ended up suppressing reforms which it had originally encouraged, such as the extension of minimum wage regulations [59]. Morgan's political study accepts that some members of the Coalition ministry, including Lloyd George himself, were sincerely committed to reconstruction in 1918 and that for a few months they carried the day; but they largely represented the remains of the 'New Liberals' and proved weaker than the conservative coalitionists once the slump began [75, *83–4*].

Gilbert argues that the Coalition government was indeed composed of businessmen who used politics to further their own interests, but these interests were narrow sectional ones [40, 24]. The commercial insurance companies, acting as a highly organised pressure group, had shaped the 1911 National Insurance Act. They handled a large proportion of all national insurance policies, and they also distributed maternity benefit to the wives of insured men, while at the same time acting for themselves by selling policies on the lives of the newborn infants. The companies therefore opposed any suggestion that the new Ministry of Health should, by encouraging the provision of public health services, maternity clinics and the like, interfere with their own access to working-class customers [39, *Ch. 3*].

The insurance companies were not the only forceful lobby. The Boards of Guardians, who administered the Poor Law, wished to maintain local control over health care for the poor, particularly in the hospitals and institutions which had been built from local rates. They also argued that they possessed a unique personal knowledge which enabled them to judge individual claims for poor relief [40, *118ff*]. Apart from these interest groups, both of which had vociferous supporters in Parliament, certain politicians and administrators had the power to hold up proposals for reform until the momentum had slackened; the most notorious obstructor being W. Hayes Fisher, President of the Local Government Board, who effectively blocked reform of the Poor Law. The BMA also objected to any extension of a salaried public medical service which would undermine private practice [52, *34*]. Out of these opposing forces the hybrid Ministry of Health finally emerged in 1918, incorporating the Poor Law administration without significant changes, and leaving the administration of health insurance to the private companies.

As the first Minister of Health, Addison tried to effect changes which he had long desired. In 1920, the Dawson committee recommended a complete reorganisation of the medical services, with doctors serving in local health centres to assist in prevention as well as cure. The hospital system, which was an unco-ordinated mixture of voluntary, municipal and Poor Law institutions, should be rationalised, though the committee trod carefully in this sensitive area. Dawson was opposed by an overpowering combination of the Treasury, which would not have stood for the expense of such a plan, the BMA, which resisted any proposals to curtail the freedom of the profession, and the voluntary hospital movement, with its numerous political patrons [1, *290ff*].

All these interest groups had been active during the war: in the postwar turmoil which reshaped the British party system, they were able to press their claims with even greater vigour. Health reform was killed in its cradle: the slump was only incidental in ensuring that health policies would be pursued without effective central direction in a system divided between private insurance, the Poor Law, municipal schemes and charity.

Other impulses were also lost even before the end of war. The government failed to make effective plans to deal with unemployment, even though temporary unemployment was expected once the war ended. In 1911, compulsory unemployment insurance had been imposed on certain trades such as shipbuilding, which had irregular employment patterns, and contributions were paid by the workman, his employer and the state. Unemployment benefit, which was set at a level even lower than outdoor poor relief, was intended only to tide the workman over short periods of unemployment, not to support him for any length of time. During the war, the most obvious measure seemed to be the extension of insurance to the whole workforce, as was strongly recommended by William Beveridge [47, *256*]. In 1916, another National Insurance Act attempted to bring most of the war-related industries under this cover. Yet in January 1918 only 200,000 extra workers were insured, instead of the 1.5 million intended.

Like industrial tribunals, unemployment insurance failed because it was opposed by many trade unions as well as employers. Beveridge blamed short-sighted unions for leaving so many workers exposed at the end of the war, without any reserve fund having been built up to deal with the post-war emergency. This explanation has usually been accepted [40, *56*], though qualified substantially by Whiteside, who argues that the government's plans were ill-conceived, especially as they offered benefits lower than in some existing trade union schemes; neither did the state scheme deal effectively with industries which went on to short-time or work-sharing during trade recessions [103]. The plan also undermined the influence of the unions, which were already uneasy at the intrusion of the state into the workplace and the dilution of labour.

Hostility from the labour movement was compounded by divisions within the bureaucracy. The Ministry of Labour would have preferred a scheme which left some autonomy to industry, and hence to the unions. But the Treasury resisted this, fearing that unemployment funds might be diverted to strikers if unions had any control over benefits. Both wanted the costs of unemployment to be covered by a fund which was self-financing, but with the war ending, soldiers returning, and workers leaving the munitions factories, rising unemployment made this impossible. The government had only two choices: to pay direct, uninsured benefits to the unemployed, or to resort to the much-hated Poor Law. The latter was unthinkable in a country still moved by patriotic sentiment, and so the unemployed received an emergency 'donation'. Although the donation was hardly generous, it came closer to the Poor Law idea of a subsistence allowance rather than the very low flat-rate benefits of pre-war insurance: it was therefore more flexible than the pre-war system in dealing with long-term unemployment, especially as benefit, like poor relief, soon came to include allowances for each dependant [40, 59]. The government had made an irreversible decision to take responsibility for the unemployed.

The Coalition government looked desperately for a plan that would make unemployment insurance pay for itself, but was hampered by its own lack of statistics. In 1920 the Unemployment Insurance Act extended insurance to nearly all workers with the important exceptions of agricultural labourers and domestic servants – poorly paid occupations with little unemployment. By this time it was too late. The amount raised through insurance contributions was not enough to fund the benefits to the growing number of unemployed; the Treasury was therefore forced to supplement the insurance fund. Neither could the government withdraw benefits from those who had not paid enough insurance contributions. The 1920 Act limited the period of insured benefit to 26 weeks in any year, but this was plainly a relic of the 1911 notion of temporary cover, irrelevant to the long-term unemployment which was developing in the depressed areas. Throughout the 1920s a series of more than 20 unemployment Acts tried to maintain a distinction between those who were entitled to insurance benefit and those who were receiving 'uncovenanted' benefits, but this division was artificial [19, 311].

Health, unemployment and industrial relations policies were in difficulties before the end of the war, but post-war conditions undermined the two areas of policy where the government had promised most finance: education and housing. Both received large grants from the state and were then savagely cut back, and it is here that the development of the 'Treasury view' has seemed most significant. H. A. L. Fisher's Education Act of 1918 was one of the most ambitious and idealistic of all the reforming measures and, unlike the erratic unemployment policies, had been planned for some years in advance. The Act offered more free places in secondary schools to scholarship winners from the working class; it allowed an expansion of the teaching profession to reduce the pupil–teacher ratio; and initiated the Burnham scale for teachers' salaries, making the profession more attractive and self-respecting. The Geddes axe cut away at the number of free places, and although it was then impossible to revoke the increased salaries which had already been granted, the numbers of teachers were reduced so that large primary classes of 50 or more were not uncommon in the cities. The government would have gone even further and raised the age of school entry from 5 to 6 had not a surge in Labour votes in by-elections caused a retreat. Historians have found little explanation for these reversals apart from a blinkered search for economies and pressures from the business class for lower taxation. Few members of the government appear to have been seriously committed to extending secondary education, which they regarded as a social luxury [88, *37–51*; 75, *290*].

The failure of the housing programme, which was the crucial test of the government's intentions, is more problematic. Addison's Housing and Town Planning Act of 1919, which gave a generous state subsidy to local authorities to encourage housebuilding, was halted with only two-fifths of the projected half million houses completed. The most controversial provision of the 1919 Act was that the Treasury would bear the cost of house construction if this involved the local authorities in raising the local rate by more than a penny in the pound, though local projects had to be approved by the Ministry of Health. Since building supplies and skilled labour were in short supply after the war, the private sector competed with the public for scarce resources. Rents were still fixed lower than a free market would have permitted, and so the cost of housing was bound to be considerably more than could be recouped from rents. The cost of the housing subsidy caused a political uproar, and in the summer of 1921 the programme was virtually abandoned. Bowley's major study, which was published in 1945 with the obvious intention of drawing lessons for the use of another post-war generation, concluded that the Act had been a failure because of its expense, and that the expense had been largely due to bad administration. Not only had the government offered a blank cheque to local authorities to build, but it had not maintained 'efficient administrative control of the use of resources' [13, *35*].

Abrams more sweepingly condemns the government's reluctance to interfere with the market in order to reduce costs, since 'home rule for industry' was the order of the day [2]. The building unions were a further obstacle, for they refused to accept dilution of skilled labour, having had long experience of the sudden fluctuations of demand in their erratic trades [76, *111*]. When the effects of government policies are examined in the localities, even greater weaknesses of planning come to light. Bowley assumed that the government had made an almost unlimited commitment to provide finance, but had not guaranteed supplies of essential materials. In fact local authorities encountered great difficulties with finance. They had to raise large capital sums for building before any subsidy could be claimed, but were deterred by a shortage of liquid capital and high interest rates, which the government had provoked by its 'dear money' policy of November 1919. The Act produced a chain of responsibility for housing: government would not give subsidies unless local authorities had provided their own share of the finance; authorities would not give advances to contractors; contractors began operations with inadequate capital and numerous bankruptcies resulted. Not surprisingly, builders preferred the lucrative private sector [65]. Wilding also argues that Bowley exaggerated administrative difficulties, when the basic policy was at fault. Since the building industry was taking much higher profits from repairs and industrial construction than from house-building, neither dilution of labour nor controlling the price of materials would have solved the problem – labour and materials would have continued to flow into the private sector. The government would have needed to intervene in the market in an unprecedented way to remedy the situation [106].

An original and seductive argument for the failure of housing reform has been put forward by Swenarton, who sees housing policy as a direct response to working-class unrest, an 'insurance against revolution'. His evidence is the government's response to reports of Bolshevik stirrings early in 1919; the way in which the housing programme was rushed through without adequate preparation; the virtual unanimity in Parliament over it; and particularly, the design of the houses themselves [93, 77–87]. The 'homes for heroes' were, by working-class standards, well-constructed and spacious, often with gardens, to show the working class the progress possible under capitalism. The new houses were not intended for the poor, who could not afford the rents, but for the respectable, organised section of the working class who were most likely to cause trouble if their discontents were ignored.

Swenarton's thesis rests to some extent on the government's reaction to the reports of unrest, which may not have been taken seriously. Neither is the point at which the government dropped the housing programme very easily related to the shifts of labour unrest: Swenarton argues that housing was not publicly abandoned until after the Triple Alliance had proved itself unable to agree on an all-out strike in April 1921 [93, 132]. Yet Addison had already been defeated in November 1920 over a bill which was intended to speed up housebuilding, while at the same time the Chancellor was asking for major cuts in all departments [76, 127]. It is doubtful whether the government could at that stage have decided that Labour would offer no further threat – nor indeed did this possibility disappear until after the General Strike. If the threat of revolution did impel government into action over housing, then it was a very short-lived threat. Swenarton's thesis may explain how the government persuaded the 'hard-faced men' to vote so meekly for Addison's Act, and also may explain the elaborate design of the houses, which were to become the most desirable bargains in the sale of council houses in the 1980s.

Recently, the word 'inevitable' has reappeared in relation to the failure of reform [75, 93], and historians have once more emphasised the economic crisis. Peden takes Fraser to task for assuming that the political will which financed the war should have been kept alive to finance reform [36, 178]: Peden stresses instead that the war was funded by borrowing rather than taxation, and that the redemption of short-term government debts after the war helped to foster an inflationary consumer boom which created competition for resources [80, 53]. The boom further convinced the Treasury of the need for balanced budgets and high interest rates as a means of controlling the economy and preparing for a return to the Gold Standard, and its powerful influence was set against social expenditure.

The failure of reconstruction shows the difficulties of trying to separate the political, economic and administrative factors which make social policy. Hypothetical questions or comparisons with 1945 might also demonstrate this. Had the political base of the government in 1918 been stronger, without the constant need to conduct internal negotiations, it might have taken a tougher line over social policy, especially as by 1921 the budget was in surplus and the cost of building materials falling rapidly. The cartoonist Low usually drew the Coalition government as a two-headed ass, 'without pride of ancestry or hope of posterity', occupied in biting itself. This left the ministries who were responsible for social policy in a weak position, never sure of political backing and vulnerable to the claims of the Treasury. Hence Addison and his housing programme were sacrificed by Lloyd George for the sake of political expediency.

Yet the alarming fluctuations of the post-war economy cannot be minimised as an influence on social policy. The one factor which unites nearly all historians in explaining the events of these years is the growth of Treasury control and the strength of the Treasury's views on economical government. The economic crisis weakened the advocates for reconstruction in the Coalition government and exposed them to more conservative interests. These were more compelling forces than the fear of revolution, which had flickered briefly in 1918–19 but which was not sufficient either to divert government plans or to prevent reforms from being whittled down in 1922. The government did not want a head-on confrontation with the trade unions, but the unions were in any case more anxious about pay cuts and dilution of labour than about rising to defend homes for heroes.

Peden's comments on the effects of war on social policy are judicious, as he argues that any conclusions will depend on whether a long- or a short-term perspective is taken [80, 56]. The post-war consensus in favour of national regeneration was brief, but the war nevertheless produced long-term effects, if only because of the ratchet-like nature of social policy. The policies which failed most irrevocably were those concerning industrial relations, which commanded little support from either side of industry. State housing and education, although far short of the ideal, had popular appeal and could not be abandoned entirely. Fraser has argued that the war accelerated the process of state intervention which had already begun [36, 177], and this is indeed borne out by the expanded state bureaucracy which the war produced, and the much higher proportion of GNP allocated to social policy after the war. Yet the war diverted policy as well as accelerating it: two of the most expensive policies, housing subsidies and the payment of doles to the unemployed, would hardly have arisen as they did without the impact of war.

Finally, the war demonstrates that the relationship between social change and social policy is not simple. The war did not produce the kind of social levelling that could bring about consensus for far-reaching reform, but it did ensure that future social policy was conducted in a more cautious fashion. The previous century had seen dramatic policies, such as the 1834 Poor Law, which dealt savagely with large groups of people, but after 1918 such policies were no longer possible. Public opinion did not make social policy, but could raise powerful objections to it. The economic changes brought about by war had a much more profound effect on social policy, but were slower to reveal themselves. Not wartime planning, but the unplanned response to economic crisis was to dominate interwar policy. The effects of war on policy should therefore be sought less in the period 1914–22, which is too short to demonstrate them, than in the interwar period as a whole.

4 Social Policy in the 1920s

(i) UNEMPLOYMENT POLICY

Unemployment is the problem which dominates the history of interwar social policy. Comparison of very dubious unemployment date before 1914 with more abundant but still unsatisfactory interwar data has led historians to two different conclusions: that interwar unemployment was, except in the very depressed years 1921–22 and 1931–33, no worse on average than before 1914 [10, *614*]; or alternatively, that even the lowest interwar rate of unemployment was higher than the highest pre-war rate [7, *443*]. A more cautious, if discouraging, approach might indicate that the statistics are not good enough to sustain either comparison [39, *59*]. Interwar governments, however, saw unemployment as a more pressing problem than it had been before 1914.

Here it becomes impossible to separate social policy from more general economic policy. The way in which interwar governments perceived their own powers over the economy limited their social strategies. Since government still doubted whether it could effectively 'manage' the economy through budgetary devices, it followed that social policy must give way to economic priorities [87, *119*]: the need to balance budgets, keep down income tax and service the National Debt all pointed in this direction.

Until at least 1927, governments interpreted the causes of unemployment in traditional terms: that Britain was experiencing a temporary downturn in the trade cycle which would shortly reverse itself, and that meanwhile unemployment was being exacerbated by inflated post-war wages [90, *171*]. If wages were reduced, more workers could be employed. Hence Baldwin's government was not disposed to block the employers' attack on wages, particularly in the struggling heavy industries. The return to gold in 1925, which raised the price of British exports, made wage reductions seem even more necessary for industries which were desperate to cut their costs. Plans for reducing unemployment which required heavy expense, such as public works, were dismissed as counter-productive. The Labour governments had some sympathy for the Fabian idea of public works in a time of slump, but saw them less in economic than in social terms as a temporary mopping up of the unemployed to prevent demoralisation. Lacking an economic rationale, suggestions of public works were vulnerable to criticism that they would take funds from more productive private invest-ment in the economy, thus 'stealing work from the future'.

While the influence of J. M. Keynes was at its height in British economic thought after the Second World War, historians who considered the relations between economic and social policy be-lieved that the problems of the depression had been made worse by government decisions. Winch showed how failure to adopt Keyne-sian methods had vitiated interwar unemployment policy: Keynes did not produce his *General Theory* until 1936, but for many years he had been attempting to wean governments from outmoded econo-mic ideas, and had recommended deficit financing of public works to generate employment [107, *Ch. 6*]. The Treasury, however, clung to financial orthodoxy, sustained by leading contemporary econom-ists such as A. C. Pigou, Henry Clay and Edwin Cannan, for whom writers of the comfortably Keynesian 1960s had scant praise. Hancock wrote of Cannan, 'it is impossible not to be appalled by the naivety and conservatism of some of his utterances, emphasized, as they were, by frequent repetition' [44, *308*]. Winch found the opposition to Keynes so astounding that he concluded darkly: 'When so much ingenuity is used to support inaction, it is to be suspected that the true grounds for opposition lay hidden deeper' [107, *118*]: the real reason was the Treasury's obsession with private enterprise as the only saviour of the economy.

In the 1970s, as Britain experienced the alarming combination of inflation and rising unemployment, the reputation of Keynes as the fount of all sound ideas on unemployment began to waver. Historians had already begun to debate whether the interwar years were as desperate for the economy as had been previously assumed [3]: now they also questioned whether Keynesian policies would have worked in any case. Hancock, who criticised 1920s policy along Keynesian lines, had recognised that the Keynesian emphasis on generating demand to stimulate employment would not necessarily create enough demand in the regions where unemployment was

41

highest, but he put his faith in 'generalized excess demand' [46, *114*]. This did not satisfy critics in the 1970s who noted that demand might well be stimulated in the more prosperous parts of the country without reviving the depressed areas [10, *630*]. Britain was two economic nations: Keynesian theory would not integrate them.

With these modern problems in mind, historians were prepared to make allowances for policy-makers in the 1920s. It seemed that policy had been determined less by traditional economic theory than by pragmatic considerations [98, *3*]. The Treasury view was reassessed not as intractable conservatism, but as a realistic approach to the difficulties facing any project of public works. In Britain, even the building of a road required protracted negotiations between local authorities, landowners and other interested parties. By the late 1920s, the Treasury believed rather that Britain's ills would be cured by rationalisation of the failing industries, since industrial efficiency was seen as a more important problem than unemployment [79, *176*]. Even Pigou and his colleagues received some commendation for having a more sophisticated grasp of regional difficulties than had been appreciated [21].

Much of the criticism of government policies in the 1920s centres on decisions which, although intended to stimulate the economy, did nothing for the unemployment problem. Chief amongst these was the return to gold, with its devastating effects on the export industries. Yet the government had believed that a stable exchange rate would benefit the international economy and restore Britain to its former position as an exporting nation. Policies which were more directly aimed at reducing unemployment were limited in both their intentions and their effects. The Unemployment Grants Committee, set up to meet the first onset of unemployment in 1920, gave government subsidies to local authorities which were prepared to undertake labour-intensive public works, but these grants were hedged around by numerous conditions relating to the local levels of unemployment and the type of works undertaken. It has been estimated that by 1929 these schemes, mainly roadbuilding, had employed on average only about 4 per cent of the unemployed [45, *108*], while local authorities in the depressed areas were the least likely to have capital available for public works.

By 1927, although the expected upturn in the trade cycle had begun, it was very patchy. Recovery was slow in the staple industries, where unemployment remained higher than in other parts of the country, and the regional nature of unemployment became obvious. Baldwin's government recognised this by setting up the Industrial Transference Board in 1928, offering removal expenses and training schemes to encourage migration from the depressed areas. This plan obviously assumed that there was still work to be had in the favoured parts of the country – an assumption which was seen to be weak even by the middle of 1929. The uncertain chance of employment in another region was not enough to attract the hard core of the unemployed, especially men aged 45 and over, away from their homes and friends, nor were they easily employable elsewhere [45].

If government theories of unemployment were traditional, their administrative policies towards the unemployed were radical [24, 53]. Mass unemployment was an emergency: the state responded by breaching the tradition of local responsibility for the unemployed, and supporting them from national taxation. The unemployment Acts of the 1920s involved the state in an apparently open-ended commitment to the unemployed and their dependants, without the apparatus of the workhouse test or stoneyard labour which was the central feature of the English Poor Law. But old fears had not died. Would the coming of the dole weaken the moral fibre of the unemployed and discourage them from looking for work?

Contemporary writers, not surprisingly, were divided in their answers to this question. Eveline Burns, in her rigorous statistical study of the insurance system, found no evidence that it had encouraged voluntary unemployment, since she argued that the level of benefit was well below the average level of wages [19, 257]. Bakke's sociological survey of Greenwich, an area of casual rather than structural unemployment, showed the great lengths to which the unemployed went in their search for work, spending many hours of the day in fruitless tramping [5, 142]. The Pilgrim Trust's later description of the long-term unemployed in English towns noted that life on the dole might seem attractive to low-paid workers with large families, because there was little margin between wages and the dole, but that surprisingly few of the long-term unemployed took this view. They pointed to the geographical and age-linked structure of unemployment, with the probability of finding work being much reduced for older workers [83, Part III].

Such arguments did not satisfy contemporaries like Cannan or Davison, who regarded the unemployment figures as unnecessarily inflated. Since unemployment benefit for insured workers was payable for periods of unemployment as short as one day, employers in industries with irregular demand could use insurance to subsidise casual or short-time wages. Dock labour, with its irregular patterns of work, and the textile industries, which had long used work-sharing devices during slumps, were the most obvious examples. Here the unemployment figures were higher than they should have been because of a large number of short-term claims for benefit. Davison also argued that administrative attempts to discourage the uninsured from claiming discretionary benefits were unsuccessful [7, 71; 29, 4].

While memories of the 1930s were still strong, and while Keynesian ideas dominated discussion of the subject, the voluntary unemployment thesis received little attention. It was revived in the 1970s by Benjamin and Kochin, who commended Cannan's interpretation and produced further econometric arguments to prove that the rate of benefit for much of the interwar period was relatively high in relation to average wages. This, they claimed, together with easy access to short-term insured benefits, encouraged a greater degree of 'search' unemployment – men would not take the first job offered but would wait for something better to turn up – and the 'OXO' system in certain industries (one day on, one day off, one day on). The lower rate of youth unemployment, attributed to the lower rate of benefit for those under 18, was further proof that unemployment could be benefit-induced, since the young had less incentive to be unemployed. Hence unemployment stayed high even during recovery in the late 1920s and late 1930s; over the interwar period as a whole, the unemployment rate would have averaged one-third lower if benefits had been equivalent to the flat-rate benefits of 1913 [7].

Benjamin and Kochin's work has been attacked on every ground from the econometric to the sociological: like Andrzjewski's military participation ratio, it provokes a ritual onslaught in most discussions of social policy, not least because of its obvious implications for the present. Since the argument rested mainly on data for benefits and wages, much discussion centred on the accuracy of these, and whether aggregate national figures had much relevance to an unemployment pattern which was perceived as sectoral and regional [23]. Even if Keynes' arguments on aggregate demand now command less support, his use of the multiplier is still used to show

44

how long-term unemployment in the staple industries led to regional unemployment in many other trades. Similarly, the young suffered less from unemployment not because of the low benefits, but because of their low wages: people between 14 and 18 were attractive to employers as cheap temporary labour: indeed, such employers obstructed plans to raise the school-leaving age [38].

In fact, Benjamin and Kochin do not deny the reality of structural unemployment, but argue that this was less important than the longer-term effects of benefits which encouraged temporary unemployment. They claim not only that benefits were high in relation to wages, but that benefits were easy to obtain. In the 1920s, local administration was in the hands of Employment Committees, composed of employers and trade unionists, over whose selection the Ministry of Health had some control. An unemployed man who had paid insurance contributions was entitled to a period of benefit; but those who did not qualify, or who had exhausted their insurance cover, received discretionary benefits. The committees could refuse discretionary payments, leaving no option but family help, charity or poor relief.

Gilbert accepts that the value of benefits rose as prices fell during the 1920s; he emphasises the fear of unrest which caused government to keep subsidising the insurance fund, and prevented it from reducing relief scales [40, 32]. Deacon, looking at the local working of the system, concludes differently: that the government's early fear of unrest was soon dissipated, and that the regulations were then operated as tightly as possible to prevent 'abuse' – a movement of policy 'from concession to coercion'. The numerous unemployment Acts of the 1920s were not designed to reduce unemployment, but to restrict access to benefits. The 'genuinely seeking work' clause was the favoured device, forcing the unemployed to produce written evidence that they had approached several employers to ask for work. From 1924 it was applied to the insured and uninsured alike. The regulation was defended by all the governments of the 1920s on the grounds that it prevented married women from seeking benefit when they were not really looking for work, and that it distinguished the 'genuine' unemployed from the scroungers. By 1927, nearly 20 per cent of applicants were being refused benefit for one reason or another, and the rate of refusals varied erratically across the country [30; 31]. In the 1930s the means test was used instead, also making access to benefits uncertain. The point is that benefits in the interwar period were so unpredictable that voluntary unemployment would not be a rational choice. Even if benefits were only marginally lower than wages, people on low incomes would find that the difference increased their hardship, a point to which Benjamin and Kochin seem insensitive [42, *346*].

Much confusion is caused by authors who use the words 'insurance' and 'dole' interchangeably. Statistics of unemployment are drawn from 'insured workers', but this means only that the workers belonged to trades where insurance was compulsory, not that individual workers had paid enough contributions to qualify for unconditional benefits [39, *173*]. In the 'search' theory, insured are more important than uninsured benefits, since the insured worker could usually claim benefit after a short waiting period. Until more thorough analysis of unemployment patterns in different trades is offered, it would be unwise to generalise on what workers 'expected' to receive when they became unemployed. In fact the system was so complex that the National Unemployed Workers Movement devoted much of its time to advising those who had been denied benefit [51].

The voluntary unemployment thesis is most convincing when applied to irregular trades such as dock labour, where the OXO system could be used by employers to keep down their wages bill. The men, who were insured, operated 'three days on the hook and three days in the book'. Wartime plans for decasualisation were not pursued, since the surplus workers would only swell the numbers of unemployed [82, *Ch. 6*]. Hence the OXO system suggests that unemployment was a 'real' not a 'voluntary' problem. Neither should historians ignore the reminiscences of the man on the Jarrow omnibus, who persists in blaming interwar unemployment on shortage of work rather than generosity of benefits.

(ii) THE CRISIS OF LOCAL GOVERNMENT

In all these efforts the state still left much discretion to local authorities and to individual choice. If, like Mussolini, the state had devised a national plan of public works, it would have needed to demolish the whole British tradition of decentralised government. No peacetime government was prepared to suggest this. Even so, a new pattern of local government emerged out of the experience of the 1920s.

Confrontation between central and local government was one of the most important unplanned consequences of the war. As we have seen, during the war the share of central government expenditure on social policy grew rapidly [78, *108*]. The First World War was less remarkable than the Second in encouraging this shift, but the longer-term effects of war, such as the housing subsidies, affected the interwar figures. At the same time, more local finance was coming not from local rates, but from central government grants: such grants were 30 per cent of local government expenditure in 1920 (comparable to the pre-war figure), but had risen to 40 per cent by 1939 [78, *200*]. Most of the grant was for specified purposes such as housing, but in 1929 the Local Government Act, through the device of the block grant, moved considerable sums from central to local government without prescribing how they should be spent.

The new financial structure had two implications. If central government subsidised rates from taxation, some of the national income could be distributed from the richer parts of the country to the poorer. At the same time, government might demand more control over local policy, even though local authorities were responsible for administering the funds. The economic problems of the time encouraged central control, since local authorities in the depressed areas were in a constant state of financial crisis, and government came to distrust local relief policies. The Local Government Act, which emerged out of several years of theatrical conflict between government and a small group of local authorities, was one of the most important pieces of legislation of the twentieth century, beginning a long process of centralisation.

The extension of unemployment insurance had less effect on the depressed areas, where many workers relied on discretionary payments because they had not been in work for periods long enough to claim insured benefits. Where these were refused, the Poor Law came into increasing use. Even those receiving benefit might also have to apply to the Poor Law for extra aid, for example if a member of the family were ill. Between 1922 and 1927, the national proportion of the unemployed who were receiving poor relief fluctuated between 9 and 25 per cent [19, *53, 343*], but the proportion in the areas of high unemployment ran well above the national average. The unemployed were also more likely to need other free services such as school meals. Unemployment, therefore, undermined local authority finances.

The local authorities which distributed poor relief were still very small, being clusters of parishes (unions) in England and Wales, and single parishes in Scotland. Even before 1914, hard-pressed authorities had been arguing that government should equalise the burden of unemployment across the country; after 1918 this demand erupted into a series of well-publicised battles associated with the London borough of Poplar, but which also broke out in several mining communities in north-east England and south Wales.

The Poplar guardians, mainly from the radical wing of the Labour party, refused to operate the strict means tests of the Poor Law, and argued that relief should be paid according to need. They rejected the basic Poor Law principle that relief should always be below the level of wages. Poplar was a very poor borough whose difficulties arose less from structural unemployment than the traditional difficulties of low pay and casual employment. Like other poor areas, it resented paying high rates to cope with its social problems when wealthy areas had few paupers and low rates. Open-handed policies inevitably led to a high relief bill and indebtedness. The Poplar borough councillors, most of whom were also Poor Law guardians, won an effective psychological battle by allowing themselves to be imprisoned on a technical charge, essentially over their demand for subsidies from the wealthier parishes of London. In the nervous days of 1920, the government responded by further redistribution of funds between London parishes, and allowed guardians to arrange Exchequer loans through the Ministry of Health. As a result, several authorities fell into even worse debt, while ignoring the relief scales recommended by the Ministry. During the General Strike and the coal strike which followed, the Poor Law became a sensitive political issue, with some unions offering generous relief to strikers' families, others trying to use the regulations to force strikers back to work [87; 27, *103*].

The rights and wrongs of Poplarism have been much debated, especially since confrontation between governments and local authorities with different political views is by no means at an end. The Labour leaders were embarrassed by Poplarism, and the foremost critics were the Webbs, who blamed Poplarism for increasing pauperism both by encouraging scroungers and by subsidising employers who used the Poor Law as a make-weight for casual earnings [99, *906*]. The defenders of Poplarism argue that the guardians, unlike the government, were trying to confront two basic problems: that work was simply not available to many of the unemployed, and that wages were too low for many families to live on [15, *118*]. In this view, Chamberlain was trying to preserve the principles of the nineteenth-century Poor Law in inappropriate circumstances, at the cost of much local suffering [87, *79*]. The Webb's figures, showing that pauperism in Poplar was far higher than the local unemployment rate warranted, indicated that the fundamental issue in the Poplar dispute was not unemployment but low wages.

With the labour movement weakened after the General Strike, Chamberlain could push through measures to consolidate the powers of central government [99, *912*]. These have been interpreted either as a political manoeuvre by the Conservatives against Labour [27, *102*], or as an example of Chamberlain's zeal for efficient administration: since the government was providing ever more finance for local authorities, it should be able to call the tune [40, *220*]. It was not only radical unions which were causing trouble, but certain Conservative ones like Sheffield, where the relief bill for the unemployed produced a heavy debt in spite of tough administration. The Board of Guardians (Default) Act of 1926 allowed the government to replace with its own nominees guardians who were in difficulties for reasons not approved by the Ministry: three Labour-controlled boards were soon suspended.

Chamberlain's disciplinary zeal went further in the Audit Act of 1927 and the Emergency Provisions Act of 1928. The former gave the auditors more power to prevent reckless local expenditure. The latter was the first taste of Chamberlain's strategy for local government: small and obstreperous councils were swamped by a larger and more powerful authority. Here the London County Council, regarded in those days as a moderate body, took over most of the financial powers of the London parishes.

The Local Government Act of 1929, with its Scottish counterpart, abolished the guardians and the Scottish parochial boards, and handed over their duties to the county and borough councils: this was the climax of Chamberlain's strategy to enlarge and rationalise local government. Public health, municipal hospitals, police, education, administration of the Poor law and unemployment assistance, with all the other complex functions of the local authorities, were now devolved to specialised committees of the enlarged councils. The Webbs and other reformers had long supported such a change in the interests of more efficient local government [55, *89*], since a larger local authority would be able to provide more expensive and wider-ranging services. On the other hand, pauper votes would have little weight in larger authorities, and could no longer be used to 'corrupt' local government by electing Poplarist councillors [32]. The 1930s have been seen as a period of comparative peace between central and local authority [55, *165*] but, as will be seen, government was not satisfied until the 1934 Unemployment Act ended local responsibility for the unemployed.

(iii) POVERTY, HEALTH AND HOUSING

The battles of Poplarism were fought not only over unemployment, but over poverty and low wages, which always confused the issue of unemployment relief. The Poor Law principle that relief should never exceed earnings, had often been hard to enforce, and the dole added further complications, since it was considered wrong that pauperism should seem more attractive than insurance benefits, or that either should be more attractive than earnings, however low. Information on poverty was not as systematically collected as the statistics of unemployment, and definitions of poverty were inevitably shifting and subjective. Poor Law statistics were intended to record destitution, not poverty, and interwar governments attempted little analysis apart from some family budget surveys of the late 1930s. Historians have relied on several unofficial surveys, all of which define poverty in different ways [63, *49*]. Rowntree's original method was to set a very low standard for primary poverty, which was defined as inability to meet essential food requirements. Living standards had risen during the war, and interwar surveys of poverty consistently showed the improvement compared with the previous generation; Rowntree's second survey of York, conducted in 1936, revealed that primary poverty had declined to 6.8 per cent of the population compared with 15.4 per cent in his pioneering survey of 1901 [86, *120*].

Chamberlain attacked poverty in 1925 through his Widows', Orphans' and Old Age Contributory Pensions Act. This extended the 1911 principle of contributory insurance: all those wage earners who paid national health insurance now paid extra contributions to entitle them and their wives to a pension of 10s a week after age 65. Previously, old age pensions had been means-tested, and were given only to those aged 70 and over. The new insurance payments also covered widows and dependents under the age of 14. Such payments, although plainly a relief to many, were hardly enough to lift their recipients above poverty or Poor Law subsidies if they were the only source of income.

All social surveys agreed that a large proportion of the poor, probably around a half, were children under the age of 14: the larger the family, the higher the risk. The campaign for family allowances was led by Eleanor Rathbone's Family Endowment Society, formally established in 1924. Many prominent people, including Beveridge, supported it, but in spite of its efforts, family allowances did not become national policy until 1945. Why did the campaign fail? Land argues that it could not succeed until it was seen to be in the economic interests of government: this happened during the first years of the Second World War, when allowances could be used to reduce inflationary pressures on wages [43, *228*]. Macnicol dates the weakening of bureaucratic resistance earlier, from 1935, when the insurance fund was in surplus and the government was being pressed to raise the level of benefits [63, *123*]. One of the main inconsistencies of the benefit system was that large families might sometimes gain more from relief, which was scaled according to the size of families, than from earnings; investigations by the Ministry of Labour in the 1930s failed to reveal that this was a serious problem, but it continued to exercise the minds of administrators. By this stage, family allowances offered a way of maintaining work incentives, while enabling government to sidestep the problem of low wages.

The struggle for family allowances also demonstrates that pressure groups are less likely to succeed if they are unable to gain a firm political base. Eleanor Rathbone could not allay the Labour movement's fears that family allowances would enable employers to keep down wages. Neither were the campaign's priorities clear, especially on the question of means tests. Eleanor Rathbone, under the contradictory influences of the eugenics movement, tried to convince her opponents that family allowances would simultaneously diminish reckless breeding amongst the working class and encourage a desirable increase in the middle-class birthrate. The

51

Treasury was not convinced that the benefits of family allowances would outweigh the expense. Feminism was Eleanor Rathbone's most consistent motive: she never wavered in her demand that family allowances be paid directly to mothers, thus giving them some financial independence. Hence the financial opposition to family allowances was reinforced by powerful traditions which favoured both patriarchy and the responsibility of the family, rather than the state, for child welfare [43, 227].

Pressure groups also influenced health policy in the interwar period, since the insurance companies and the BMA were both vitally concerned. Under the 1911 National Insurance Act, insured workers received some income in times of illness, and could have the free services of a panel doctor, but the system was much criticised. Only lower wage earners (under £250 a year from 1920) were eligible for state-subsidised insurance, and not their families. Insurance was arranged through a multitude of approved societies, from huge commercial companies like the Prudential to smaller friendly societies or trade union schemes. In this competitive world, the commercial societies necessarily tried to keep their national insurance funds in surplus, but took in all comers, using their contacts with the working class to sell private policies. The friendly societies were more interested in providing a wide range of insurance benefits, but to do this they had to keep in surplus, and so refused to take bad risks. Gilbert and others have alleged that the very success of the commercial companies after 1911 effectively undermined the tradition of mutual aid societies run by the working class themselves. Although older friendly societies like the Odd-fellows participated successfully in the system, their management began to resemble that of the commercial companies: by the end of the interwar period less than a dozen large societies catered for nine-tenths of the insured population [40, 301]. Friendly societies and commercial companies divided the insured between them, accounting for about 45 per cent each, with smaller trade union and all other organisations taking the rest [105, 170].

Gilbert stresses the conservative role of the commercial insurance companies, who built up surplus funds from national insurance during the war and refused to pool them with the less successful companies [40, 258]. Surpluses, which had to be applied for the benefit of the insured, were used to offer extra inducements, such as dental treatment, to gain members. Yet pooling, as recommended by the Royal Commission on National Health Insurance in 1926, was the favoured way to finance the extension of insurance cover to dependants. Since many working people could not afford to pay extra insurance premiums for their families, pooling seemed the only answer as long as government refused to finance the extra burden out of taxation. Less attention was paid to extending insurance than to deterring 'malingerers', especially married women workers who, it was said, tended to claim health benefits whenever they needed a day off work to take care of children.

The conservatism of the companies was reinforced by government economy: the Exchequer contribution to the insurance fund fell from £10m to £6m between 1921 and 1930, even though the amount paid out in benefits had risen from £28m to £36m. Defending their position led the companies to become one of 'the most formidable of parliamentary interests' [40, *296*, *261*]. Gilbert sees the insurance companies as a major obstacle to improving the insurance system during the interwar period. Whiteside, however, casts them as scapegoats for government parsimony. In the late 1920s health insurance came under strain as tighter administration of unemployment benefit pushed many of the unemployed towards claiming sickness benefit: at this stage the surpluses of many of the smaller insurance companies were wiped out. While cutting its own subsidy to health insurance, the government allowed the unemployed to continue receiving sickness benefits during the first year of unemployment, and the cost was borne largely by the societies. When national insurance was well in surplus during the early 1920s, the companies had not opposed plans for extending it to dependants. It was government, now obdurately determined to retrench, which refused to extend health insurance [105].

The debate on the role of pressure groups should not obscure some of the more fundamental shortcomings of the insurance system. As Whiteside comments, even if the societies' surpluses had been pooled, there would not have been enough funds to meet the needs of the working population. Indeed, the Ministry of Health seemed more interested in the finances of the system than in its efficiency. The steady downward trend of infantile mortality and the major infectious diseases encouraged a certain complacency which was to be more rudely challenged in the 1930s.

The panel system allowed the workman more regular access to his doctor, and offered a better standard of treatment than the Poor

Law medical service had done. If a workman did not have to pay for his own treatment, he could afford more medical attention for his family; and many doctors were reconciled to panel service when they found that not only did it reduce their losses from bad debts, but also brought them as private patients the families of their panel patients [34, *144*]. The insured were entitled to drugs and simpler appliances, but hardship occurred if members of their families needed expensive or long-term treatment.

The annual capitation fee which the panel doctor received for each insured person on his list caused much dispute between the BMA, the insurance companies and the government. Immediately after the war, the government raised the fee, lowered it again in 1922, and announced a second cut in 1923 at the demand of the approved societies. The BMA responded by threatening the resignation of 97 per cent of all panel practitioners, and the government, caught between two influential factions, gave way to the doctors: the capitation fee was not lowered [40, *273*]. Nevertheless, the medical profession was divided in its attitude towards the health service. The panel, which had aroused much suspicion in 1911, was largely accepted, but many doctors objected to plans to extend the system, either by including dependants, or raising the income threshold for insurance. The profession resisted the possibility that they might become the salaried employees of the state [52, *Ch. 8*]; some because they made a fair income from private practice, others because they had gloomy memories of salaried employment under the Poor Law or the friendly societies, which had paid them badly and restricted their professional freedom.

In 1911 the doctors had been afraid that laymen on the local insurance committees would be able to interfere with their methods of treatment. The committees were anxious to prevent malingering, and also to ensure that the doctors were not providing fancy special treatments for which extra fees would have to be paid. Eder's research indicates that after early disagreements the system worked relatively smoothly, with medical judgements being left largely to medical referees rather than to laymen. The capitation fee did not encourage the panel doctor to offer more than basic treatment to his patients, but since in those days there were relatively few drugs of proved efficacy, this was probably no disadvantage. Although the division of the medical profession between GPs and hospital consultants was already apparent, the GP still 'stitched hands, set

bones, pulled teeth, gave out dietary information and . . . prescri-
bed tons of cod liver oil' [34, 187]. The panel system's effects on the
national health were problematic, since it was hardly able to deal
with the chronic ill-health associated with poverty, but the system
stabilised medical incomes, made some form of medical treatment
available to most working people, and greatly enhanced the prestige
of the medical profession.

Other aspects of health administration were mostly left to the
discretion of local authorities during the 1920s, but the small rating
areas produced great inequities. Both school meals and school
medical services were only as good as local conditions permitted.
The imposition of a penny rate in an impoverished area might
produce less than half the amount per child than the same rate in a
wealthier part of the country [53, 185]. Some of the areas of highest
unemployment offered the cheapest and least nutritious meals
[102]. The Board of Education regarded school meals not as a
health measure, but an educational one. Children from poor
families received free meals only if the school medical officer
believed that their ability to learn was being diminished by
underfeeding. Yet the doctor's judgement was often based on a few
minutes' cursory examination of the child [100, 118]. Government
subsidies to the system were very limited, and the Board's attitude
restricted the number of free meals to the lowest possible.

Provision of public hospitals also depended on the attitude and
income of local authorities, and whether the government gave
subsidies. In 1911, public authorities had provided about 1,300 beds
in sanatoria for tuberculosis: by 1929 there were about 15,000 beds.
Maternity hospitals, which also received a government grant for
their construction, expanded rapidly [1, 352]. Without government
aid, progress was slower, notably in the treatment of the mentally
handicapped. In violation of the intentions of the 1913 Mental
Deficiency Act, many patients were left in Poor Law hospitals and
workhouses rather than sent to specialised institutions [27, 98].

The hospital system was patchy and lacked co-ordination. The
power of the medical profession was growing: doctors and nurses
objected to working in badly equipped and understaffed hospitals,
and in many towns both the municipal and the Poor Law authorities
tried to bring their hospitals up to modern standards. County
councils and rural Poor Law guardians, dealing with much smaller
populations, often had neither the will nor the finance to provide

more than simple cottage hospitals, while chronic cases could end up in workhouses which had changed little since the nineteenth century. There was no logical division between the public and the voluntary sector; both had originally existed only for the poor, but many voluntary hospitals now charged fees and took in patients from the wealthier social classes who appreciated that the large voluntary hospitals now offered the best treatment for acute illnesses. There was much overlapping of functions between the various hospitals; from the patient's point of view, the nature of his hospital, and the standard of treatment, was something of a lottery.

Histories of health services in this period usually concentrate on the provision of hospitals and trained staff: an alternative view of medical history suggests that social policy has been too much influenced by the elitism of the medical profession, which gives greatest respect to the curative rather than the preventive services [35]. The chief threat to the health of the working class was poverty, and a shifting of the debate from medical politics to wider issues might be desirable.

The construction of low-cost housing in the 1920s also depended on a mixture of central subsidy and local option. Once Addison's generous subsidies had gone, more depended on local initiative. Chamberlain's Housing Act of 1923 offered a lower annual subsidy of £6 per house over 20 years, and gave private builders preference over the councils. Unlike the homes for heroes, Chamberlain's houses were restricted in size and cost. His policy failed to attract private builders, who found it more profitable to cater for the growing demand for home-ownership among the middle classes. Wheatley's Housing Act of 1924 shifted the subsidy back to council houses, and increased it to £9 in urban and £12.50 in rural parishes over 40 years. His concordat with the unions led to a more rapid rate of construction, as can be seen from the figures in Table 2.

Bowley's densely factual account of housing policy assumed that government policy was a series of pragmatic experiments, which could be judged in terms of their success in solving the housing shortage. Housing policy in the 1920s had only one consistent aim: to expand the housing stock as fast as possible, with the Conservatives after 1924 reluctantly accepting that councils rather than private builders were the most effective providers of housing for the working class [13, *40*]. Melling criticises Bowley for presenting housing policy as an abstract administrative problem rather than the

Table 2 House-building 1919–1934 (000s of houses)

	Private enterprise	Local authority	Total
Addison subsidy	170.1	43.7	213.8
Chamberlain subsidy	362.7	75.3	438.0
Wheatley subsidy	15.8	504.5	520.3
Unsubsidised	1085.8	—	1085.8

Source: [41, *223*; 13, *271*].

focus of tense local conflicts and political passion [68, *11*]. Housing became one of the Labour Party's main claims on the support of the working-class electorate, and although the Conservatives began to remove rent controls in 1923, and later cut back on Wheatley's subsidies, they could not avoid government responsibility for housing.

Criticisms of Bowley's approach overlook two of her most forceful points, which have underpinned many studies of housing policy. Firstly, Bowley recognised that rents and low wages were the unsolved problem at the heart of housing policies. Secondly, as a consequence of this, housing policy was beset by regional disparities [13, *133*]. Both these problems were clearly revealed during the 1920s, when the effects of government housing policy were 'regressive', in that the rents of even the cheapest council houses were higher than the poorer sections of the working class could afford. New council estates tended to be occupied by skilled and white-collar workers, leaving behind the poor, especially those with large families, in overcrowded and insanitary slums. Government assumed that these problems would be solved as the poor moved into the houses vacated by better-off workers, but the number of new households, being formed in the 1920s was as high as at any time during the nineteenth century, and house-building barely kept pace with demand [41, *228*].

The regional problem was more diffuse, being the result of both local financial problems and social factors such as age and class structure. Areas with much poverty and unemployment, especially those with a long history of bad housing, gained proportionally less from the housing subsidies than more fortunate cities. Smaller towns in Wales, Durham and Lancashire were faced with an uncertain future and possible emigration of their population. The unemployed could not afford council rents, and ratable values were low, just when social problems were putting greater pressure on the rates. Great disparities resulted: in favoured Sussex, the combination of public and private house-building had by 1931 satisfied all but 7 per cent of the estimated housing requirement of 1921: in county Durham the shortfall was 32 per cent [13, *131, 111, 66*].

Recent research on interwar housing has begun to explain in more detail why the localities reacted in such different ways to government housing subsidies. Local politics and power struggles led councils in different directions, not only in the rate of construction, but in the quality and design of houses. The plans for housing estates revealed much about social expectations and class relationship (68; 28). Swenarton states bluntly that 'design is an ideological process' [93, *195*], and the new estates often showed the results not only of economies but of the planner's vision of what working-class life should be. Features which were most productive of strife were the absence of pubs from many estates, and the desire of some architects to maximise living space by having only one living room instead of the small living room and little-used parlour 'for best' which most working families preferred [93, *127*].

The main conclusion on 1920s housing, as on health care, is that the emerging pattern of two economic nations was reflected in the social services. Regional stagnation and unemployment led, in Bowley's phrase, to an Inner and an Outer Britain in which those areas most in need of social services were the least likely to get them. The main challenge to policy, as the administrators of the day saw it, was to minimise the social effects of regional decline by providing a more uniform standard of service.

5 The 'Low, Dishonest Decade'?

(i) UNEMPLOYMENT POLICY: THEORY AND PRACTICE

The years of depression from 1929 reinforced the centralising tendency in social policy. It is tempting to see this as part of a wider movement towards a managed economy, in which the government and the Treasury were slowly persuaded into a new financial world of monetary management, tariffs, marketing boards and rationalisation of industry. Attempts at management were both uncoordinated and circumscribed, but they help to define the limits of social policy in the 1930s, especially in the response to unemployment. Britain was not alone in feeling the pressures towards centralisation, but the National government did not confront a depression as severe as in America or Germany, and its preferred solutions were correspondingly less dramatic. The debate on social policy resembles the debate on economic policy, which tries to weigh economic theory against political expediency. Again it is necessary to distinguish the government's theory of unemployment from its treatment of the unemployed, although the former partly determined the latter. Unemployment could be left to prolonged economic debate: the unemployed were an immediate political problem.

In 1929 the Treasury had to deflect a vigorous attack, not from the Labour Party, but from Lloyd George's Liberals, whose election pamphlet *We Can Conquer Unemployment* promised an immediate reduction of unemployment through loan-financed public works, to cost £251m over two years. Keynes was the moving force behind this programme, and he backed it with his own manifesto, *Can Lloyd George Do It?* The electorate no longer trusted Lloyd George, but Keynes had a gift, rare amongst economists, for effective publicity. His call for reflation was lost in the crisis of 1931, with the fall of the Labour government and cuts in public expenditure, but became more compelling not only as his own argument matured, but as the

New Deal offered the example of a democratic experiment. The Treasury needed to redefine its own ideas against this challenge.

Peden and Middleton both stress the Treasury's pragmatic response [79; 70]. It accepted that government expenditure could temporarily relieve unemployment, but did not see this as the highest priority. A sharp rise in government borrowing would reduce business confidence at home and abroad, especially amongst holders of government stock. The ultimate result would be a reduction of private enterprise which would cancel out the government's activities. The stringent orthodoxy demanded of the Labour government by the international financial community in the crisis of 1931 might bear out this view of the business world. Furthermore, the limited experiments in public works carried out by the second Labour government were slow to get started, and seemed to the Treasury to have achieved very little in terms of results for expenditure. Schemes worth £110.9m were approved, to which the Exchequer was to contribute less than half, but in the first year of the Labour government the schemes actually started were worth only £44.4m, and by 1931 had given direct employment to only 61,165 people [89, *219*; 70, *165*].

By 1937, when the Treasury was accepting a budget deficit in order to finance rearmament, it still favoured planned and selective measures rather than the sledgehammer approach to aggregate demand of the early Keynesians. Both Liberals and Labour thought of public works in terms of traditional measures such as road and bridge construction, which was not necessarily fitted either to the skills, the age group or the geographical location of the unemployed. (It might be pointed out that Hitler's controversial programme of *motorisierung* was not merely for the provision of roads, but also mass production of vehicles, with a more direct spin-off to the heavy industries.)

In the event, the National government made relatively little effort to provide work for the unemployed, and its financial policies are seen as, at best, mildly reflationary [85, *151*], at worst, counterproductive [70, *Ch. 7*]. Changing interpretations of the National government's economic theories have also modified the assessment of its unemployment policy. The main questions are these: were policies towards the unemployed seriously intended to reduce unemployment; were they merely a holding operation until the economy revived; or were they palliatives for a problem which the government believed to be insoluble?

From 1929 government had better statistical information about the duration of unemployment, and it was easier to distinguish the hard core of long-term unemployment in the depressed areas from the cyclical or frictional patterns in the more favoured Midlands and South. The partial nature of the recovery was also clearly shown in that, although the total numbers of unemployed were falling, from a peak of nearly 3 million in 1931–2 to 1.5 million by mid 1937 [40, 315], the numbers of long-term unemployed continued to rise. In 1929, only 4.7 per cent of the unemployed had been out of work more than a year; in 1936 this had risen to 25 per cent [85, 157]. Unemployment was also revealed largely as a problem of the older worker, for by 1936 over a third of the unemployed were between 45 and 65 [92, 60].

It does not take long to list the National government's chief measures to increase employment. They continued the industrial transference schemes of the 1920s, hoping to encourage labour mobility, but only orderly migration was approved; anyone who took to the road in search of work (and many did) lost entitlement to the dole and encountered the sharp end of the Poor Law in the casual wards of workhouses. A small number of the unemployed was offered retraining in residential colonies, but these were popularly believed to be punitive measures against scroungers. The most serious effort came the year before an election, and after much public criticism of government inaction, in the Special Areas Act of 1934. The original government grant of £2m was for amenities such as hospitals and waterworks in the specified areas, but the effects of this were so limited that in 1937 an amending Act allowed local authorities to remit rates, rent and taxes to attract firms into the Special Areas. Fewer than 50,000 new jobs were created under the Acts [92, 65].

Addison's description of these measures as a 'pretentious imposture'[3] has been more politely conceded by several historians, who have seen them as political rather than economic in intention [72, 470; 43, 342]. More positively, such measures showed that government did appreciate the regional nature of the problem [24, 70]. But areas were 'Special' only if they satisfied strict require-ments: the unemployment rate must be over 25 per cent of the insured population, and over 40 per cent of the insured must work in the same industry. Hence Clydebank was a special area, but

Glasgow, with a rate of nearly 37 per cent unemployment among insured workers, was not. The Scottish Office pressed for a programme of industrial investment, but was rebuffed by the pervasive Treasury view in Whitehall [20].

On the other hand, the government encouraged charitable efforts which were plainly intended to palliate the social effects of unemployment, rather than attack it at the root. It gave modest subsidies to the National Council of Social Service to establish clubs which would take the unemployed off the streets. By 1935 there were around 1,300 clubs with a membership of over 150,000, and they offered all kinds of activities from sport to training in shoe repairs, or just a place to read the newspaper and keep warm [50; 83, 396]. Juvenile Instructional Centres, run by the Local Education Authorities, were also set up for the unemployed aged between 14 and 18. JICs had begun in the 1920s, but an Act of 1935 made attendance compulsory for the young unemployed – a measure which might be compared with the government's reluctance to raise the school-leaving age. The centres offered some education and training, but were particularly keen to maintain physical fitness and prevent the young from becoming demoralised. They could be legitimately regarded as temporary expedients, since the young tended to be unemployed for fairly short periods [92, 65].

The voluntary effort which went into manning and supporting charitable schemes for the unemployed might imply that public concern, led by the Royal Family, was somewhat in advance of the government's. Bruce expresses the commonly held view that the National government was simply timid and lacking in the imagination necessary to deal with an unparalleled problem [17, 266]. A government which used 'Safety First' as its election motto would be unlikely to offer dynamic policies. Alternatively, since unemployment in Britain was a more limited and containable problem than in Germany, the majority of the electorate accepted it with fatalistic resignation, and backed the National government's retrenchment policies [41, 160]. It should be remembered, however, that the voter had relatively little choice, since the Labour Party was split after 1931 and the Liberals had ceased to be a serious force in politics. The only politicians to offer a radical alternative were Lloyd George, now tainted by financial corruption, and Mosley, with his Fascist associations. In a monolithic Parliament, effective dissent would have to come from within the Conservative Party, and by the mid 1930s it was being expressed by Harold Macmillan and the 'middle opinion' group who favoured a cautious form of managed economy: their influence, however, was for the future [24, 74].

Winch suspected that the National government's attitudes were based not on timidity but on outright nihilism, since they believed that government could do little but try to stimulate private industry [107, 122]. His views have been reinforced by Miller, using Cabinet papers to argue that the 'consistent, deliberate absence of action was itself a purposeful policy' [72, 454]. Although the government expected some recovery from the slump of 1929–30, it did not believe that employment in the staple industries would increase, in which case the hard core of older unemployed would probably never work again. The government's main aim was to protect existing social and economic relationships while maintaining the strictest control over public spending; hence most of its effort was directed towards relief policy, which served the dual purpose of diminishing unrest and deflecting opposition into futile debates over details of administration. The soundness of its policy, in its own view, was borne out by continued electoral support, a degree of economic recovery, and preservation of the social structure.

Whether the government was timid, or whether it firmly believed that intervention was fruitless, its attitudes set up political tensions which give point to the notion of an 'imposture'. No political party in the 1930s could face an election if it seemed indifferent to the unemployed or unable to tackle unemployment. Palliative policies such as the Special Areas Acts were electoral window-dressing, which succeeded in political if not in economic terms because the opposition was so enfeebled. This is not to say that Chamberlain deliberately diverted opposition into focusing on his relief policy, for he did his best to remove this from Parliament altogether, but his radical approach to relief nevertheless achieved this result.

The National government had been created in the crisis over unemployment insurance, which by 1931 was in total confusion. From 1927 insured workers who had paid contributions for 30 weeks could receive benefit for an unlimited period. Those who had paid fewer contributions could still receive temporary benefits termed 'transitional' because it was expected that economic recovery would restore their ability to pay contributions. Both types of benefit were subjected to the 'genuinely seeking work' test. The uninsured, and those denied benefit, had only the Poor Law. In

1930 the Labour government's Unemployment Insurance Act abolished the 'genuinely seeking work' test, and made the Treasury directly responsible for financing transitional benefits which, since unemployed continued high, were politically important in keeping the unemployed off the Poor Law [40, *94–6*].

The rush of claimants to transitional benefit doubled their numbers to 300,000 in two months. Contemporary critics like Davison attributed it to an influx of casual and seasonal workers, married women and scroungers, none of whom were suitable for insurance [29, *9*]. A sharp drop in the numbers of unemployed on poor relief also indicated that claimants had shifted from a less popular form of assistance [19, *53*]. Consequently, a substantial charge was transferred from local rates to the Treasury. The slump played havoc with this arrangement, and by the end of March 1931 the debt on the Insurance Fund had risen to over £75m, making it the prime target of the May Committee's demand for economies. The National government's response was not only to cut benefits by 10 per cent, but to reimpose a time limit of 26 weeks on insured benefits and to subject transitional benefits – now the greater part of all benefits – to a household means test. This was to be operated by the Public Assistance Committees of the new local authorities, and brought the whole administration of unemployment relief closer to the unpopular inquisitorial methods of the Poor Law, which the committees also administered [26]. The Poor Law itself was again put under much strain in the distressed areas, since those who were disallowed benefits, or had them reduced under the means test, had to apply for supplementary poor relief. Even those on full benefit often had to resort to the Poor Law for an urgent expense, such as children's shoes [19, *313*].

Public Assistance Committees, however, were more independent than the local employment committees of the 1920s. They were often more responsive to the local electorate than to central direction, and since they were now disbursing the taxpayers' money, they did not have to be mindful of the rates. Relief practices and costs varied enormously, making the Treasury uneasy about providing funds which it did not administer. The government responded with the Unemployment Act of 1934, a major centralising measure which created the Unemployment Assistance Board (UAB) to assume responsibility for nearly all the unemployed, and set up a large bureaucacy to administer relief locally. There were to be two main categories of the unemployed: the fully insured who received benefit as of right, and those who did not qualify for insured benefit but could draw means-tested unemployment assistance. To the fully insured, the 1931 cuts in benefit were restored, reflecting the easing of the economic situation, and compulsory insurance was extended to a much wider section of the working class, including agricultural labourers. (This extension was then delayed until 1937.) The second category accounted for 42 per cent of those receiving benefit in 1935–6 [29, *129*]. A small proportion of the unemployed was left to local public assistance under the Poor Law, including both the old group of 'disreputable' poor such as vagrants, and embarrassed members of the middle class or the self-employed who had never paid contributions.

Burns saw the 1934 Act as an important step towards government responsibility for the unemployed, administratively necessary both because it resolved the chaotic local administration of benefit, and because it ended the injustice by which the most depressed parts of the county had to carry the heaviest burden of Poor Law relief to the unemployed [19, *314*]. Gilbert endorses this, arguing that the Act set a precedent for treating the unemployed according to need and, by removing them from the Poor Law, defused social tension [40, *191*]. Yet Davison's contemporary response was to regret that the government had not contented itself with reforming local administration, which he believed was at its best more flexible and economical than a central bureaucracy [19, *88*]. His view that 'not social needs, but political and financial calculations', inspired the creation of the UAB has been given a modern gloss by Briggs and Deacon, who see the UAB as Chamberlain's final assault on Poplarism, which was still flourishing in the Public Assistance Committees of the distressed areas [16]. The consequences of Chamberlain's vendetta would have been even more radical had he been permitted to carry out his original plan to remove *all* public assistance from local control and bring all socially distressed groups under a 'nationalised Poor Law'. In this he was frustrated by Betterton, the Minister of Labour, who saw greater political security in pursuing the aim of all post-war governments to keep the unemployed off the Poor Law [71].

It is usually accepted that the first experiment in centralisation was disastrous, since the government had not foreseen that many of the unemployed would receive less generous allowances under the new UAB relief scales than they had from the public assistance committees. Political considerations and popular disorders forced the suspension of the Act until 1937 in many areas, during which time the unemployed could remain on public assistance if it advantaged them. Both Chamberlain and Betterton wished to 'take unemployment out of politics', by which they meant that the UAB would have little accountability to Parliament, and that individual cases could not be raised there. Cynics may argue that governments are keenest to remove an issue from politics when it is highly contentious, and in practice the Ministry of Labour had to answer for the actions of the UAB. To defuse local complaints, the government reluctantly appointed tribunals to hear appeals from the unemployed against the level of benefit, but the odds against successful appeals were heavy, both because of the secretive and Byzantine nature of the means test, and of the strong central pressure which was exerted on the tribunals. Even so, tribunals managed to reach quite variant decisions over similar cases [62].

(ii) UNEMPLOYMENT AND SOCIAL WELFARE

Although unemployment was the most urgent issue in social policy during the 1930s, it also had implications for other social problems. The long-term unemployed were living on benefits which, even if they may sometimes have been higher than the earnings of poor families, were still at poverty level. To the questions which had been asked in the nineteenth century concerning the relationship between poverty and other social problems such as crime, disease, poor housing and infant mortality, was added the question of whether unemployment was also undermining the nation's health. Since long-term unemployment was largely confined to the depressed areas, conditions in these areas might worsen without preventive measures.

Infant mortality rates are usually accepted as a rough index to health conditions in past times, since little systematic data were collected on illnesses except for the major infectious diseases. Infantile mortality may be divided into neonatal mortality (under one month) and post-neonatal (from one month to one year old). During the first month of life, death is more likely from developmental conditions encountered in the womb, or congenital problems: after that, the baby is more vulnerable to infectious diseases or ailments such as enteritis which may be due to a poor environment. The post-neonatal rate is therefore assumed to be a more sensitive reflector of social conditions. From Table 3 it can be seen that changes in mortality during the interwar period were largely owing to changes in the post-neonatal rate.

The debate on health became heated in the 1930s, as the Ministry of Health denied that any deterioration had taken place in the depressed areas, in spite of criticisms from a radical section of the medical profession and complaints from several of the pressure groups who were campaigning for family allowances. The Ministry argued that the health services and school meals were protecting the unemployed and their families. Of course, had the Ministry decided that life on the dole was threatening the health of the unemployed, it would have been politically most embarrassing between 1931 and 1934 for a government which had just cut the rate of benefit [63, Ch. 3]. After 1934, the UAB's relief scales were the focus of criticism, the most famous onslaught coming obliquely from John Boyd Orr. His

Table 3 Infant Mortality (deaths per 1,000 live births) in England and Wales and in Scotland 1926–39

| | England and Wales | | Scotland | |
Year	Neonatal	Total under one year	Neonatal	Total under one year
1926	31.9	70.2	36.4	83.1
1927	32.3	69.7	37.1	88.7
1928	31.1	65.1	36.7	85.7
1929	32.8	74.4	37.3	86.8
1930	30.9	60.0	35.2	83.0
1931	31.6	66.4	35.8	81.1
1932	31.6	65.5	35.9	86.2
1933	32.3	63.7	37.6	81.1
1934	31.3	58.6	36.2	77.7
1935	30.4	56.9	38.4	76.8
1936	30.2	58.5	37.6	82.3
1937	29.8	57.6	38.2	80.3
1938	28.3	52.7	34.9	69.5
1939	28.1	50.4	36.5	68.5

Source: 109, 441

small book *Food Health and Income* (1936) analysed the budgets of families with different incomes in relation to current medical thinking on nutrition. His conclusion, that only 50 per cent of the population had a diet good enough to keep them in health, provoked a violent response from the Ministry and much argument within the profession. Boyd Orr was attacked for setting his nutritional standards too high, since they were based on a generous American assessment of food requirements; neither did they overthrow the view, always current in British policy, that health can be maintained on a low income if housewives spend the income wisely. The debate may have diverted attention from a less assailable part of Boyd Orr's findings: that 4.5 million people had diets inadequate in every respect, and another 9 million had seriously deficient diets [14, *49*]. The Ministry took its stand, however, on the annual statistics of infant mortality.

The current argument over these statistics mirrors that of the 1930s. Winter accepts the Ministry's contention that there was a steady downward trend in infantile mortality in spite of the depression [108]. Neither were there any unusual features in the mortality rates of the depressed areas compared with more prosperous cities such as London. The Registrar General's reports always showed great differences between the social classes: in 1930–32, of each 1,000 babies born to the lowest social class (Class V), 77 died, but in the highest social class (Class I), around 33 died, an excess of 135.5 per cent. By 1939, the figures had fallen to 60.1 per 1000 in Class V and 26.9 in Class I, an excess of 123.4 per cent [110, *246*]. Winter also points out that, in spite of much lower rates of mortality since the Second World War, the class difference has survived, with an excess death rate in Class V of 118.2 per cent in 1951. The Ministry of Health was well aware of the class difference and argued that as it had persisted since recording began in 1911, it arose from 'traditional' social conditions such as bad housing or bad habits rather than economic recession. Similar explanations were used to explain the higher rates of infant mortality in Scotland, which Winter also describes as 'traditional', though in fact Scottish rates had been lower than English ones until the end of the nineteenth century.

The relationship between infant mortality and economic conditions in a developed society is not simple, for short runs of statistics may be distorted by occasional outbreaks of infectious diseases such as influenza which affect all social classes. Winter has made the most sophisticated effort so far to subject the statistics to time-series analysis, and detects no relation between economic fluctuations and mortality at any lag from one to ten years: in theory, this should take into account not only the conditions prevailing at the time the child was born, but conditions affecting the mother before the birth [110, 245]. Winter is not a crude optimist. He does not argue that his figures show that the 1930s were a healthy period, but rather that a combination of social policy and the self-sacrificing habits of parents probably acted to protect infants from the worst effects of the depression. The tone of a later essay is more cautious than the first and cites medical research from the 1970s to show the possibility of higher infant mortality among the children of mothers who were born in the worst years of the depression. The effects of depression may be more delayed than evidence from the 1930s can show.

Winter's arguments have been directly challenged by Webster [100], who is sceptical of the official health statistics. He contends that, even if infant mortality rates were declining, the 1930s arrested a downward trend which was rapid during the first war and the early 1920s, and again after the Second World War. International comparisons showed a slower decline in mortality in Britain than in other advanced countries: by 1939, England was ninth in the League of Nations' Table of Infant Mortality, Scotland seventeenth. The dramatic effect of rationing, free orange juice and emphasis on maternal health during the Second World War also showed how misplaced was the complacency of the 1930s.

One point at issue between Webster and Winter is the usefulness of the Ministry's regional data during the 1930s. It might be argued that the rather large areas taken by the Ministry for purposes of comparison are not suitable for measuring the effects of depression except in a very crude way. If it is accepted that those in employment were enjoying rising living standards during the 1930s, then even in regions with high unemployment the majority of the workforce would share these gains, which could be reflected in the mortality rates, cancelling out adverse effects amongst the unemployed. In the absence of any statistics which compare infant mortality among the long-term unemployed with other working-class groups, small-area statistics are a better guide than larger regions, and Webster argues not only that small-area statistics for the depressed regions show more evidence of worsening mortality rates in the early 1930s, but that the Ministry actively discouraged local studies which produced embarrassing results [100, *113*].

The debate on mortality will be furthered only by careful local studies which relate small-area statistics to the local economy and also to the effectiveness of local policies. Winter's original judgement that mortality did not seem to be influenced by the political views of local authorities [109, *452*] is unhelpful in assessing the overall effect of policy on health. Labour councils, even if anxious to promote health, were often very short of money, and Webster shows that authorities in the depressed areas often offered the worst services in maternal and child welfare [102]. It might also be conjectured that Conservative authorities were not only richer, but quite likely to be impelled by humanitarianism or electoral strategy in pursuing vigorous policies: it would be unreasonable to expect local policy to divide neatly along political lines.

Maternal mortality rates, which actually increased over the interwar period, are a less obvious guide to social welfare since they are not as influenced by social class, and since many deaths were due to toxaemia, did not fall noticeably until the introduction of the new sulphonamide drugs in the late 1930s. Again, Webster is inclined to make more use of them than Winter, since a charitable experiment to provide free milk to expectant mothers in South Wales produced a drop in mortality so remarkable that the Ministry had difficulty in believing it. Only local studies of *all* the types of service available to mothers, including voluntary ones, are likely to shed light on this. Winter's rather hasty suggestion that 'both medical and paramedical care *and* the attitudes of pregnant women to it left much to be desired' [109, *456*], has been effectively criticised from a feminist standpoint by Lewis, who gives a depressing account of the maternity clinics [57]. They conducted medical examinations but could not offer treatment, and were more lavish with advice, often patronisingly given, than practical assistance. Clinics which offered free or cheap milk, crèches and sympathy were popular. Ante-natal examinations, rarely a cheering experience, were in the 1930s unhelpful and humiliating for many working-class women. Both central and local administrators were inclined to blame the higher death rates of mothers and children in Class V on the ignorant behaviour of mothers: if this were the case, then improved nutrition during the Second World War proved wonderfully educational.

Winter's later essay is closer to Webster's assessment that the mortality rates are, in any case, not sufficient guide to health or nutrition. Malnutrition did not necessarily kill, but it seriously debilitated many people. The main burden of ill-health seems to have been borne by mothers, who had no health insurance or access to the extra meals available to schoolchildren, and who were likely to take less than their share of the family rations in order to supplement their children's diet. Their welfare could be assisted by local authority services such as free milk depots, which were neither universally provided nor always offered in a manner the woman found acceptable. The health of schoolchildren also remained contentious, since the Ministry's highly optimistic statistics rested on the cursory examinations which caused some unease even within the Ministry itself [101; 63, *58*]. School medical officers who were used to working in poor areas simply set themselves lower standards than those outside; problems such as bad teeth, unhealthy physique and defective eyesight were accepted as 'normal' amongst these children.

The complex of unemployment, low pay and poor health continued to bedevil housing policy in the 1930s, although government consciously aimed to provide housing for poorer families, rather than those who could afford an economic rent. Health conditions were known to be worse in the slums, where communal privies, overcrowding and primitive plumbing made cleanliness an almost impossible goal for even the most determined housewife. Moving slum families to new estates reduced the danger of infectious diseases such as TB, but Orwell and many others commented that the higher rents could only be afforded if food budgets were reduced; again, the deprivation was mainly undergone by wives and pre-school children.

In 1930, Greenwood's Housing Act began to shift attention from increasing the housing stock to encouraging slum clearance; its subsidy to local authorities varied directly with the number of people rehoused, and was intended for the larger families which were most likely to be both overcrowded and unable to pay higher rents. It followed that local authorities would be allowed to charge differential rents, or give rebates, according to need. The new policy had an element of income subsidy which had been missing from previous legislation. Rents might be adjusted if a family's circumstances changed, as from unemployment. The National government ended the Wheatley subsidy as part of its financial economies, but its

Housing Act of 1933 concentrated on slum clearance: a return, as Bowley argued, to the sanitary priorities of the nineteenth century [13, *140*]. Since a 'slum' was very narrowly defined, mainly in terms of overcrowding, the plight of many people on low incomes and in only slightly superior housing was ignored.

Local authorities again reacted in various ways, impelled by complex political and social forces. By 1938, about 100 local authorities in England and Wales operated differential renting policies; Finnigan's study of Leeds shows the immense bitterness which these could produce. The Labour council in Leeds took the 1930 Act to its logical conclusion until 1935, and charged rent according to income; about 8 per cent of families paid no rent at all. This did not lead to good relations on the new estates, since neighbours were paying different rents for the same houses, and they also resented the weekly inquisition into their earnings [68, *Ch. 4*]. Nevertheless, the policy of the 1930s, with its growing emphasis on compulsory clearance and demolition, further encouraged the disappearance of the private landlord from the British housing market, although about half the population still lived in privately rented accommodation by the end of the period [41, *242*]. The estates, unbeautiful but well-built, had by 1939 relieved the worst pressure on housing, but the problem of quality was far from solved, as were the great inequalities between the regions.

The 1930s were obviously not lacking in social policy, some of it radical. The aspect of policy which repelled certain contemporaries was the official tendency to deny the existence of social problems, especially if they had implications for unemployment policy. For the historian, it also raises serious questions about the reliability of government statistics, particularly those on health. The National government, of course, were not to know that their policies would inevitably be compared with those of the Second World War, when national efficiency rather than financial stringency would once more become the overriding motive.

6 Conclusion

The working class which entered the Second World War could call upon the resources of the state for material support more comprehensively than their predecessors in 1914. In part, the new provision was simply an extension of legislation passed before 1914: insurance now covered such a wide section of the working class that many members of the white-collar and middle classes expressed resentment, especially over the medical treatment which they found an expensive item for themselves. Some policy was innovatory, particularly in council housing and in a hospital system which relied neither on charity nor the Poor Law. The financial problems of the interwar years also increased the state's reluctance to leave social policy to the localities – a reluctance which stemmed from political distrust as much as the attempt to reduce inequalities. In their tendency to centralise policy, interwar governments moved closer to the Welfare State.

Three decades of social insurance demonstrated its popularity with both government and recipient. Insurance could be claimed without humiliation, while government preferred its fixed commitment to the insurance fund to the unpredictable demands of 'uncovenanted' benefits. But economic crisis and the continuing poverty of many people set limits on insurance, so that large gaps remained. Once the safety-net of insurance was removed, most forms of assistance bore a close resemblance to the Poor Law, which also remained on the statute books until 1948 to deal with the most helpless of social casualties and to supplement the deficiencies of insured benefits. The household means test linked unemployment assistance to the Poor Law: it ensured that the family, rather than the state, still had the first responsibility. It was for all the excluded sections of the population that Beveridge formulated his wartime plans for universal insurance.

Although great changes had occurred in social policy, few of them had been planned. Interwar governments did not often ponder the fundamental aims of policy, but were more concerned with mopping up after each emergency. Social policy had to show some consideration of a wider electorate, but the influence of democracy was negative rather than positive. Except for a brief period at the end of the war, government felt little direct pressure, but it proceeded cautiously. Benefits once given were difficult to withdraw, but they could be cut or made more exclusive. If any lessons can be drawn from this period, they might show that social problems are also subject to the multiplier. A massive problem, such as long-term unemployment, requires not only a policy specific to itself, but puts pressure on all other aspects of social policy. Although interwar governments spent far more than their predecessors in upholding the standards of material life, much of this expense merely enabled them to mark time. If the unemployed had not absorbed so much social expenditure, what might have been possible in health, housing, or education?

The historiography of this subject is also an example of how historical explanations emerge out of their own times. Few historians would now accept that social policy has shown a linear progression towards the Welfare State. In some cases, the historiography has reverted to explanations which would gratify the shades of Chamberlain and Pigou. Social policy offers particular temptations to historians because even those who avoid theory have their own belief about what kinds of policies are desirable and how they should be paid for. The history of social policy cannot be detached from the present: historians are time-servers in more ways than one.

References

1. H. L. Beales and R. S. Lambert (eds), *Memoirs of the Unemployed* (1934), p. 112.
2. G. Orwell, *The Road to Wigan Pier* (Penguin, 1962), p. 80.
3. Quoted in W. Hannington, *Ten Lean Years* (1940), p. 154.

Select Bibliography

Place of publication is London unless otherwise stated.

[1] B. Abel-Smith, *The Hospitals 1800–1948* (1964). A pioneering survey.

[2] P. Abrams, 'The failure of social reform 1918–20', *Past and Present*, 24 (1963).

[3] B. W. Alford, *Depression and Recovery? British Economic Growth 1918–1939* (1984 reprint). A companion volume to this one. Rehearses the debate over British economic performance.

[4] S. Andrzejewski, *Military Oranization and Society* (1954).

[5] E. Wight Bakke, *The Unemployed Man. A Social Study* (1933). An account of the social effects of unemployment by an American observer.

[6] T. Barna, *Redistribution of Incomes through Public Finance in 1937* (Oxford, 1945).

[7] D. Benjamin and L. Kochin, 'Searching for an explanation of unemployment in inter-war Britain', *J. Political Economy*, LXXXVII (1979). A full statement of their controversial view that government relief policy increased unemployment.

[8] ——, 'Unemployment and unemployment benefits in twentieth-century Britain: a reply to our critics', *J. Political Economy*, XC (1982). Has not convinced their critics.

[9] A. E. Booth, 'An administrative experiment in unemployment policy in the 1930s', *Public Administration*, LXI (1978). On the creation of the Unemployment Assistance Board.

[10] A. E. Booth and S. Glynn, 'Unemployment in the interwar period: a multiple problem', *J. Contemporary History*, X (1975). See also the ensuing debate with Tomlinson, Ibid., XIII (1978) and XV (1980).

[11] ——, 'The public records and recent British economic historiography', *Economic History Review*, XXXII, 3 (1979). Salutary comments on the pitfalls of using newly-available official sources.

[12] A. E. Booth and M. Pack, *Employment, Capital and Economic Policy: Great Britain 1918–1939* (Oxford, 1985). A critical survey of the unemployment policies espoused by different political groups.

[13] M. Bowley, *Housing and the State 1919–1944* (1945). The standard account of policy, with many statistics.

[14] J. Boyd Orr, *Food Health and Income* (1936). 72 pages with devastating political implications.

[15] N. Branson, *Poplarism 1919–1925: George Lansbury and the Councillors' Revolt* (1979). A pro-Poplar account.

[16] E. Briggs and A. Deacon, 'The creation of the Unemployment Assistance Board', *Policy and Politics*, II (1973). Relates this to the background of Poplarism.

[17] M. Bruce, *The Coming of the Welfare State* (1966). Useful survey of legislation, erratically organised.

[18] Kathleen Burk (ed., *War and the State: the Transformation of British Government 1914–1919* (1982). Collection of essays on the administrative changes caused by war, including a very good one by Burk on the Treasury.

[19] E. M. Burns, *British Unemployment Programs, 1920–1938* (Washington, 1941). Essential factual account with many statistics.

[20] R. H. Campbell, 'The Scottish Office and the special areas in the 1930s', *Historical Journal*, XXII (1979). Argues that Scottish initiatives were dampened by Whitehall.

[21] M. Casson, *Economics of Unemployment: An Historical Perspective* (Oxford, 1983). Defends some of the leading interwar economists from Keynesian attacks: some are easier to resurrect than others.

[22] R. A. Chapman and J. R. Greenaway, *The Dynamics of Administrative Reform* (1980). Useful survey of developments in the civil service.

[23] H. Collins, 'Unemployment in Interwar Britain: still searching for an explanation', *J. Political Economy*, XC (1982). Attacks Benjamin and Kochin for ignoring regional and sectoral factors.

[24] S. Constantine, *Unemployment in Britain between the Wars* (1980). Useful short survey of the literature.

[25] R. Cross, 'How much voluntary unemployment in interwar Britain?' *J. Political Economy*, XC (1982). Attacks Benjamin and

Kochin for lack of administrative knowledge.

[26] M. A. Crowther, 'Family responsibility and state responsibility in Britain before the Welfare State', *Historical Journal*, XXV (1982). Argues that older Poor Law traditions were continued in unemployment policy.

[27] ——, *The Workhouse System 1834–1929* (1981).

[28] M. J. Daunton (ed.), *Councillors and Tenants: Local Authority Housing in English Cities, 1919–1939* (Leicester, 1984). A collection of essays on the local factors influencing housing in major cities. Excellent introduction.

[29] R. Davison, *British Unemployment Policy: the Modern Phase since 1930* (1938). Criticises centralisation of relief policy because of its extravagance.

[30] A. Deacon, *In Search of the Scrounger: the Administration of Unemployment Insurance in Britain 1920–1931* (1976).

[31] ——, 'Concession and coercion; the politics of unemployment insurance in the twenties', in A. Briggs and J. Saville (eds), *Essays in Labour History 1918–1939* (1977). Deacon's work gives an important reassessment of local policies, and undermines arguments about the 'generosity' of benefits.

[32] A. Deacon and E. Briggs, 'Local democracy and central policy: the issue of pauper votes in the 1920s', *Policy and Politics*, 2 (1974). Argues that the government's fear of the power of pauper votes was well-founded.

[33] D. Dilks, *Neville Chamberlain*, vol. I. *Pioneering and Reform, 1869–1929* (1984).

[34] N. R. Eder, *National Health Insurance and the Medical Profession in Britain 1913–1939* (New York, 1982). Covers both medical politics and the actual workings of the panel system.

[35] D. M. Fox, *Health Policies, Health Politics? the British and American Experience 1911–1965* (Princeton, 1986). An alternative view of medical history, stressing the influence of medical elites on social policy.

[36] D. Fraser, *Evolution of the British Welfare State* (2nd edn, 1984). Lucid and deservedly popular textbook.

[37] W. R. Garside, 'Juvenile unemployment and public policy between the wars', *Economic History Review*, XXX (1977). See also the rejoinder by Benjamin and Kochin in Ibid., XXXII (1979).

[38] ——, 'Unemployment and the school-leaving age in inter-war

Britain', *International Review of Social History*, XXVI (1981).

[39] ——, *The Measurement of Unemployment: Methods and Sources in Great Britain 1850–1979* (Oxford, 1980). Shows how statistics were collected and demonstrates their numerous pitfalls.

[40] B. B. Gilbert, *British Social Policy 1914–1939* (1970). The most sustantial account of the intricacies of policy-making.

[41] S. Glynn and J. Oxborrow, *Inter-war Britain, a Social and Economic History* (1976). More a series of essays than a sustained theme, but with a much more rigorous methodology than many textbooks. Pro-Keynes.

[42] S. Glynn and A. Booth, 'Unemployment in Interwar Britain: a case for re-learning the lessons of the 1930s', *Economic History Review*, XXXVI (1983). Questions whether the Keynesian theories of demand would have been an appropriate basis for policy.

[43] P. Hall, H. Land, R. Parker and A. Webb, *Change, Choice and Conflict in Social Policy* (1975). An admirable and widely used collection of essays on the theories of social policy, including Land's study of the origins of family allowances.

[44] K. J. Hancock, 'Unemployment and the economists in the 1920s', *Economica*, XXVII (1960). The Keynesian view.

[45] ——, 'The reduction of unemployment as a problem of public policy 1920–1929', *Economic History Review*, XV (1962). Also reprinted in [84].

[46] L. Hannah, *Inventing Retirement: The Development of Occupational Pensions in Britain* (Cambridge, 1986).

[47] J. Harris, *William Beveridge: a Biography* (Oxford, 1977).

[48] J. R. Hay, *Origins of the Liberal Welfare Reforms 1906–14* (1975). A companion volume to this one, giving the pre-war background to social policy.

[49] ——, *The Development of the British Welfare State 1880–1975* (1978). Useful textbook, with a selection of documents.

[50] R. Hayburn, 'The voluntary occupational centre movement, 1932–39', *J. Contemporary History*, VI (1971).

[51] ——, 'The National Unemployed Workers' Movement, a reappraisal', *International Review of Social History*, XXVIII (1983).

[52] F. Honigsbaum, *The Division in British Medicine 1911–1968* (1980). Thorough, if stilted, account of medical politics.

[53] J. Hurt, 'Feeding the hungry schoolchild in the first half of the twentieth century', in D. S. Oddy and D. S. Miller (eds), *Diet and*

Health in Modern Britain (1985). Shows the limitations of the school meals system.

[54] H. Jones, 'Employers' welfare schemes and industrial relations in inter-war Britain', *Business History*, XXV (1983).

[55] B. Keith-Lucas and P. G. Richards, *A History of Local Government in the Twentieth Century* (1978). Includes an essay on Poplarism.

[56] I. Levitt, 'The Scottish Poor Law and Unemployment 1890–1929', in T. C. Smout (ed.), *The Search for Wealth and Stability* (1979).

[57] J. Lewis, *The Politics of Motherhood: Child and Maternal Welfare in England 1900–1939* (1980). Stimulating account of health conditions and the attitudes of policy-makers to working-class women.

[58] R. Lowe, 'The Ministry of Labour 1916–24, a graveyard of social reform?' *Public Administration*, LII (1974).

[59] ——, 'The erosion of state intervention in Britain 1917–24', *Economic History Review*, XXXI (1978).

[60] ——, 'Bureaucracy triumphant or denied? The expansion of the British civil service, 1912–39', *Public Administration*, LXII (1984).

[61] ——, *Adjusting to Democracy: the role of the Ministry of Labour in British Politics 1916–1939* (Oxford, 1986). Important study of the theory and practice of bureaucracy in the modern state.

[62] T. Lynes, 'Unemployment Assistance tribunals in the 1930s', in M. Adler and A. Bradley (eds), *Justice, Discretion and Poverty* (1976). On the inconsistencies in the system of tribunals on unemployment benefits.

[63] J. Macnicol, *The Movement for Family Allowances 1918–45* (1981). An absorbing account which raises important general questions about social policy.

[64] A. Madison, 'Origins and impact of the welfare state, 1883–1984', *Banca Nazionale del Lavoro Quarterly Review*, 148 (1984). International comparisons of the economics of welfare.

[65] S. Marriner, 'Cash and concrete: liquidity problems in the mass production of "Homes for Heroes"', *Business History*, XVIII (1976).

[66] T. H. Marshall, *Social Policy* (3rd edn, 1970). Much used survey of the principles of British social policy.

[67] A. Marwick, *The Deluge: British Society and the First World War*

(Penguin, 1967). Good on the social changes which influenced policy.

[68] J. Melling (ed.), *Housing, Social Policy and the State* (1979). Attacks Bowley's administrative approach and sets housing in the context of class struggle.

[69] D. Metcalf, S. J. Nickell and N. Floros, 'Still searching for an explanation of unemployment in inter-war Britain', *J. Political Economy*, XC (1982). Econometric attack on Benjamin and Kochin.

[70] R. Middleton, *Towards the Managed Economy: Keynes, the Treasury and the Fiscal Policy Debate of the 1930s* (1985). A subtle study of the relationships between politicians, bureaucrats and economists. Good bibliography.

[71] F. M. Miller, 'National Assistance or unemployment Assistance – the British Cabinet and relief policy 1932–3', *J. Contemporary History*, IX (1974).

[72] ——, 'The unemployment policy of the National Government 1931–36', *Historical Journal*, XIX (1976). An important article on the contradictions between the economic nihilism and political rhetoric of the 1930s.

[73] ——, 'The British unemployment assistance crisis of 1935', *J. Contemporary History*, XIV (1979).

[74] A. S. Milward, *The Economic Effects of the Two World Wars on Britain* (2nd edn, 1984).

[75] K. O. Morgan, *Consensus and Disunity: the Lloyd George Coalition Government 1918–22* (Oxford, 1979). Gives weight to the seriousness of the reforming impulse, and outlines the forces which overwhelmed it.

[76] ——, *Portrait of a Progressive: the Political Career of Christopher, Viscount Addison* (Oxford, 1980). Tries to rescue its subject from long-standing charges of political ineptitude.

[77] C. L. Mowat, *Britain between the Wars 1918–1940* (1955). Impressive general history which puts social policy into its context.

[78] A. T. Peacock and J. Wiseman, *The Growth of Public Expenditure in the United Kingdom* (Princeton, 1961).

[79] G. C. Peden, 'The "Treasury view" on public works and employment in the interwar period', *Economic History Review*, XXXVII (1984).

[80] ——, *British Economic and Social Policy: Lloyd George to Margaret*

81

Thatcher (1985). Stresses the economic constraints on social policy.

[81] G. Peele and C. Cook (eds). *The Politics of Reappraisal* (1975). Series of essays including Beloff on the role of the higher civil service and Stevenson on 'the politics of violence'.

[82] G. Phillips and N. Whiteside, *Casual Labour: The Unemployment Question in the Port Transport Industry 1880–1970* (Oxford, 1985). Considers the long-standing problem of underemployment which has received less attention than it should.

[83] The Pilgrim Trust, *Men Without Work* (1938). An assessment of the social effects of unemployment from the viewpoint of the charitable trusts.

[84] S. Pollard (ed.), *The Gold Standard and Unemployment Policy between the Wars* (1970). A collection of seminal articles.

[85] ——, *The Development of the British Economy 1914–1980* (3rd edn, 1983). The standard economic survey.

[86] B. S. Rowntree, *Poverty and Progress: a Second Social Survey of York* (1941).

[87] P. Ryan, 'The Poor Law in 1926', in M. Morris (ed.), *The General Strike* (Penguin, 1976).

[88] B. Simon, *The Politics of Educational Reform 1920–1940* (1974). A depressing account of political apathy towards education.

[89] R. Skidelsky, *Politicians and the Slump: The Labour Government of 1929–1931* (Penguin, 1970). Splendid political narrative with much comment on social and economic policy.

[90] ——, 'Keynes and the Treasury view; the case for and against an active unemployment policy in Britain 1920–1939', in W. J. Mommsen (ed.), *The Emergence of the Welfare State in Britain and Germany* (1981).

[91] J. Stevenson, 'The making of unemployment policy 1931–35', in M. Bentley and J. Stevenson (eds), *High and Low Politics in Modern Britain* (Oxford, 1983).

[92] ——, and C. Cook, *The Slump: Society and Politics During the Depression* (1977). Concentrates particularly on labour and unemployment.

[93] M. Swenarton, *Homes Fit for Heroes* (1981a).

[94] ——, 'An insurance against revolution; ideological objectives of the provision and design of public housing in Britain after the First World War', *Bulletin of the Institute of Historical Research*, LVI (1981b).

[95] P. Thane (ed.), *The Origins of British Social Policy* (1978). A useful collection of essays on different aspects of policy, including Ryan on Poplarism.

[96] ——, *Foundations of the Welfare State* (1982). Includes international comparisons.

[97] R. M. Titmuss, *Essays on the Welfare State* (1963).

[98] J. Tomlinson, *Problems of British Economic Policy 1870–1945* (1981). Disputes the importance of economic theory in policy-making, especially towards unemployment.

[99] S. and B. Webb, *English Poor Law History, Part II. The Last 100 Years* II (1929). Still the most substantial account.

[100] C. Webster, 'Healthy or Hungry Thirties?' *History Workshop*, XIII (1982). The pessimistic view.

[101] ——, 'The health of the school child during the depression', in N. Parry and D. McNair (eds), *The Fitness of the Nation: Physical and Health Education in the Nineteenth and Twentieth Centuries* (1983).

[102] ——, 'Health, Welfare and unemployment during the depression', *Past and Present*, 109 (1985).

[103] N. Whiteside, 'Welfare legislation and the unions during the first world war', *Historical Journal*, XXIII (1980a). Sees wartime insurance plans as an attack on the union movement. See also comments by Lowe in Ibid., XXV (1982).

[104] ——, 'Industrial welfare and labour regulation in Britain at the time of the First World War', *International Review of Social History*, XXV (1980b).

[105] ——, 'Private agencies for public purposes: Some new perspectives on policy making in health insurance between the wars', *J. Social Policy*, XII (1983). See also the ensuing debate with Honigsbaum, Ibid., XII (1983).

[106] P. Wilding, 'The administrative aspects of the 1919 housing scheme', *J. Social Policy*, LI (1973).

[107] D. Winch, *Economics and Policy: A Historical Study* (1969; Fontana, 1972). Lucid exposition of developments in economic thought from the Keynesian viewpoint.

[108] J. M. Winter, 'The impact of the First World War on civilian health in Britain', *Economic History Review*, XXX (1977).

[109] ——, 'Infant mortality, maternal mortality and public health in Britain in the 1930s', *J. European Economic History*, VIII (1979). The optimistic view.

[110] ——, 'Unemployment, nutrition and infant mortality in Britain, 1920–50', in J. M. Winter (ed.), *The Working Class in Modern British History* (Cambridge, 1983).

[111] ——, *The Great War and the British People* (1985). Wide-ranging study of the effects of the war on living standards.

Index